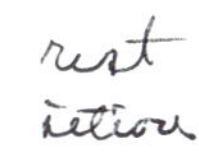

The Original BASEBALL GOLF SWING METHOD

Train your body to play great golf using the natural motions of baseball

DON PETERSON
with **PHIL NERO**

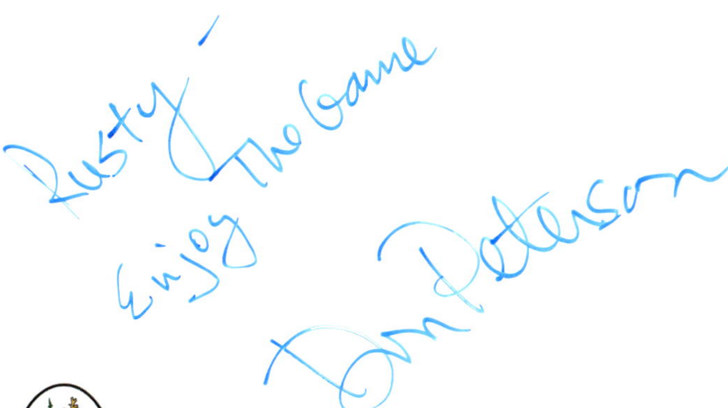

Singing River Publications, Inc.

The Original Baseball Golf Swing Method

ISBN - 10 digit: 0-9789870-3-9
13 digit: 978-0-9789870-3-9

Published by

Singing River Publications, Inc.
PO Box 72
Ely, MN 55731
www.singingriverpublications.com

Author/writer: Don Peterson with Phil Nero
Design/Graphics: Jeff Zmania, Zman Designworks

Printed and bound in Canada

In memory of Charles Jackson Berry – a great friend and constant source of inspiration, confidence, and wisdom

I am one of many people influenced by Jack Berry. People were naturally drawn to him. Jack didn't always talk a lot. He was a person who motivated you with a look. When he spoke you listened and took note. For example he'd say, "Don, you've spent your entire life learning to play golf and now learning to teach it. Write it down. People will pay for your knowledge." Jack gave the hardest time to the people about whom he cared. A great "needler," one of Jack's favorite lines was: "Well, you've got the talkin' done."

Thanks to you Jack, now I do.

I would also like to thank my wife Sharon, who gives me love, my son Cade Jackson Peterson, who inspires me, Jack's wife Mary Ann Berry, who gives me direction, A.C. and Betty Eddy for their devotion, and Joe Segal for his friendship.

A final thank you goes to my mother and my father who allowed me to play golf.

– Don Peterson

In appreciation of my wife, Meredith, and children, Adam and Stephanie, for their tolerance, support, and generous love. Thanks also to David McCraw and Bob David for helping to keep this project alive.

And in recognition of the golf companions who would make up my dream Asa Ole Open field: Bob Morrison, Karl Klein, Rob Gehman, Joe Giardullo, Joe Spadaro, Denny "Zen Bud" Darmek, Billy Stanton, Gene Laczniak, Tony Kane, George Young Jr., Brian Downs, Andy Donato, Mike Andolina, Mike Kuchta, Jeff Browne, Brian Harriss, Dick Rice, Lea Campbell, and Samir Amin.

– Phil Nero

We would also like to thank Ken Sanders and Dan Foster of the Major League Baseball Players Alumni Association and many of its other members who, along with professional golfers Todd Hamilton, Tim Simpson, and Rick Rhoden, took time to consider and endorse the principles of the *Baseball Golf Swing Method*. Special thanks too for the creativity and professionalism of Jeff Zmania of Zman Designworks and Chris Moroni of Singing River Publications.

Thank you to The PGA Tour SuperStore of Buckhead, Georgia for the use of their indoor training area, and to our models Mike Davie, Cam O'Donnell, Tom Haire, and LaDonna Smith.

THE DRILLS

The Original BASEBALL GOLF SWING METHOD

FOREWORD

BY DAVEY JOHNSON

***The relationship between baseball and golf goes back to the early glory years of our national pastime.* Close ties between the personalities of both sports and a growing awareness of similarities in the athletic fundamentals of both games have continued to grow in the decades since.**

Consider Mildred Ella "Babe" Didrikson. Born in 1911, she is perhaps the greatest female athlete of the 20th century. She earned her nickname because of the many home runs she hit playing baseball while still a child. Sports enthusiasts know her too as "Babe" Zaharias because she married professional wrestler George Zaharias in 1938.

She won a silver and two gold medals in the 1932 Olympic Games, the same decade she took up golf. She went on to win 55 amateur and professional events, among them the 1946 U.S. Women's Amateur tournament. In 1947 she became the first American to win the British Women's Amateur tournament, and won 17 titles in a row that year. As a professional she won 10 majors including the U.S. Women's Open in 1948, 1950 and 1954.

Her baseball namesake, George Herman "Babe" Ruth, whom she met years after first sharing his name, was also an avid golfer. No doubt they compared notes on the similarities between the baseball and golf swings, as Ruth was also known to do with a fellow named Sam Byrd.

Byrd was a lesser-known Yankees outfielder who roomed with The Babe and learned a lot from Ruth about hitting. Babe emphasized the importance of connecting the lead shoulder and arm to the body. This allows the shoulders and larger muscles of the abdomen and legs, not just the arms, to power the ball. In baseball this is commonly referred to as keeping the lead shoulder in – a very important swinging and hitting technique.

While not especially well known as a baseball player, Byrd went on to make a unique mark on the PGA Tour. He adapted what Ruth told him about hitting and, along with his own studies of other notable hitters of the era, adapted that knowledge for his golf game. Was he successful?

Yes. In the 1940s, Byrd became the first and only major league baseball player to ever win an event on the PGA Tour. His multiple wins include the 1945 Texas Valero Open. Like the authors of this book, he believed that the baseball and golf swings are almost identical, except for the swing plane.

In 1960 Byrd met a then relatively unknown golf instructor called Jimmy Ballard and became his mentor. Ballard is renowned today as a teacher of many professionals. Moreover, a baseball hitting drill

Babe Ruth taught Sam Byrd back in the 1930s persists to this day in the golf world. Babe used to place a towel under his arm to keep his shoulder in and his lead arm connected to his body. Vijay Singh is among a number of pro golfers you will see doing this on the practice range today.

The connections go on. Sam Snead and Ted Williams were business partners in a fishing gear company. How would you like to have been a fly near the bait bucket when those two started talking hitting techniques?

Former all-star pitcher Rick Rhoden became a Celebrity Tour standout who has also made an impact on the PGA Champions Tour. Watch international big league wunderkind Ichiro Suzuki swing today. Observe how he uncoils his core, propels his arms with centrifugal force, and even transfers his weight forward (as all golfers do) to get a running start to first base.

The Original Baseball Golf Swing Method teaches that the athletic motions involved not only with hitting a baseball, but throwing a baseball as well, can be incorporated into building a sound, athletic, repeatable golf swing.

This book is not the first time someone has made the baseball-golf swing connection. However, this presentation of drills, concepts, and training routines is likely the most comprehensive connection yet. The drills are designed specifically to give you a working knowledge of the golf swing and the ability to execute it with power and precision.

If you're like me, you've probably absorbed hundred of golf tips and advice over the years. However, Baseball Golf does more than give you a lot of information. It puts that information together in a way designed not just for gaining knowledge, but for realizing results. The former allows you to understand the swing, correct your mistakes, and continue to improve. The latter allows you to play golf better.

In short, this book is truly an exciting, fulfilling journey into golf swing execution and awareness.

Davey Johnson
June 2007

Davey Johnson is a four-time All-Star, a three-time Gold Glove winner, and the 1997 American League Manager of the Year.

He hit 43 home runs for the Atlanta Braves in 1973, breaking Rogers Hornsby's all-time mark as second baseman. He managed the New York Mets to the 1986 World Series Championship.

His baseball knowledge and athleticism also translate to success on the golf course, where he carries a 2 handicap and regularly competes on the Celebrity Players Tour.

Take Me Out To The Baseball Golf Game

ABOUT THE ORIGINAL BASEBALL GOLF SWING METHOD

The athletic golf swing – many teaching pros talk about it, and most have some method for teaching it to aspiring golfers. But unless you have a golf-lesson bankroll that could finance a year of college and time to spend at a high-tech academy, very few teachers can do little more than take the average player and plunge him or her into an overwhelming world of confusing swing thoughts and conflicting theories.

Factor in software that allows any instructor with a camera and a computer to dissect the swing with a cobweb of lines, and we see how an overabundance of well-intended advice (some valid, some not) contributes to an overload of information.

Too often the effect on the golfer standing over a ball is a state of mind in which the athletic swing is lost to paralysis by analysis. The average person's hope for an athletic, instinctive ability to swing smoothly and with tempo sinks into an all-too-familiar quagmire of reverse pivots, off-balance swings, and mis-hits – by products of too much muscle tension and advice overkill.

Don Peterson has a simple approach that navigates common obstacles and leads you step-by-step to a sound, athletic golf swing. I know because it worked for me in ways I would not ever have dared imagine if not for an odd series of events. My path to Don, while not in the mystical league of Bagger Vance and his authentic swing within, has a unique twist.

The journey began in the waning days of 2004 with winter setting in, a time when we Midwest residents of Cheeseville and Badgerland take our games inside large tents with high ceilings and wonderful heating systems. They are commonly known as golf domes – giant canopies for grand hopes and lofty aspirations. Here we dream of taking our swings and games to new heights. Come spring,

or mid-winter getaway, our games will be greatly improved. Such grand delusions have seen me through many an otherwise unbearable winter.

The perfect Milwaukee winter Sunday for me is an early church service, followed by a coffee-to-go en route to the Currie Park Golf Dome. December 26, 2004, seemed like many other such Sundays. This one, however, held a special, late Christmas present – the discovery of hidden roots to an athletic golf swing of my own.

It came about a half hour into a practice session. Maybe I bent more than usual at the waist and knees. Maybe my grip was looser. Maybe my muscles relaxed at the same time. Whatever the reason or combination of factors, the swing felt great. It was pure and clean. The ball jumped high and fast, taking a soaring, driving arc that I rarely enjoyed watching – at least when *I* was swinging a golf club.

There was something more. The swing felt fluid and natural. Oh, I had made some fairly good swings now and again. But as a 20-plus handicapper, no swing – not even the one with which I hit my only 280-yard drive – felt anything like that swing on that day. Something about it felt hauntingly familiar, owned by me somewhere else, almost in some other time. Then it came to me.

It would be fun to say what I discovered was from a previous incarnation on some misty golf course. It might be fun to write a novel about how I went into a meditative state, became friends with that other spirit self, and induced him – even better, her – to occupy my body and go on to win the U.S. Open. That would be fun. But fortunately for the world of fiction, the swing was my own, linked to a less-inhibited part of me in this life. It was, believe it or not, a bent-over kissing cousin to my baseball swing. I was never a great baseball player, but I played a year of college ball. I was far more adequate at the national pastime then, than I've ever been at passing time on the links.

An exciting journey into swing ensued for about a month after that day in the golf dome. I developed a personal philosophy based on the belief that the baseball swing is the golf swing on a different plane. To reclaim my baseball swing and incorporate it into my golf game, all I would have to do is swing the club as if I were going after a knee-high fastball and, bent at the waist, try to hit everything to centerfield. I went back to about a half dozen swing concepts from baseball and adjusted them for golf. I worked at them and found I had completely eliminated my reverse pivot. Other good things followed.

Then one day I approached a local pro from whom I had taken a number of lessons and asked if he had ever considered doing an instructional video. He listened while I explained what I had been working on and asked to see the results. His eyes lit up when he saw the difference in my swing, and I began drafting a script titled *Baseball Golf: Reclaiming Your Baseball Swing for the Links.* My enthusiasm, or at least hopes for originality, crashed halfway through the script when I stumbled on Don Peterson's web site. He too had been delving into the mystery of what he called "*Baseball Golf*."

Slowed but not stalled, I called this teaching pro from outside Atlanta. And while the cell phone connection was clear, the concept connection was unfathomably better. This voice from the digital network was the yang to my *Baseball Golf* yin. For every personal concept I shared with him, he had a related idea and a drill that not only helped develop it further, but could explain why what I was trying to do should and does work.

This book is about more than how our two golf worlds collided. It's a product of what was formed after they did. There was a bond of shared enthusiasm between a golf teacher who possessed the formula for an athletic golf swing and a writer/hacker with a vague understanding and intuitive belief in the secret to the formula, along with a desire to express it in a way that could be understood and demystified. If you read this book and practice what it teaches, our collision will rock your golf world in ways you cannot begin to imagine.

Don Peterson and I met face to face for the first time in spring 2006 near General Mitchell International Airport in Milwaukee. The in-person connection was as solid as our initial contact. He left town and promised to send me some material he had put together. About a week later, a plain envelope that looked like it had been kicked around the postal system for years arrived at my home. Inside were pages of an old, beat up manual he had compiled – weathered, unbound photo copies.

My first impression was that much of the material was superfluous. In my mind, developing a *Baseball Golf* swing didn't require such a formal approach with so many drills. After all, I had uncovered the hacker's Holy Grail, a simple concept that would demystify the golf swing and make a solid, repeatable swing easy to attain. My "discovery" could eliminate the reverse pivot, poor balance, and many nagging flaws, allowing the average golfer to stand over the ball with greater confidence, swing with more power and accuracy, and even shave a couple of strokes off his or her score. You could say I suffered from Bagger Vance Syndrome. I wanted that swing within, and I wanted it magically.

Baseball Golf is about a different kind of swing within. The *Baseball Golf Swing Method* morphs the hitting motion and skills of baseball with the throwing and pitching motions of baseball and morphs them again into the golf swing. The result is the balanced, athletic *Baseball Golf* swing I desired. I got a glimpse of this morphed swing that December day when I felt it for the first time.

Don's drills paved a longer road to what I was seeking, not a tediously long one, but not the quick fix I had in mind. And in my mind, the *Baseball Golf* swing was indeed a fast track through the land of woods and rough to a haven of fairways and greens. That was my mindset when we made plans to meet again in Georgia.

As luck would have it, we met in the middle of a heat wave, 90° plus with a 110° plus heat index. My swing was already wilting in the weeks before our meeting. When we went to a range it melted into ugliness. I thought it was just a matter of bad timing. In reality it was perfect timing. The truth is, when you're banging around in the high 90s, a couple of strokes and a hot round here and there do not comprise the Promised Land. Moreover, while you can reclaim your baseball swing for golf, once you do reclaim it, you must learn to repeat it without letting your old swing flaws compromise the motion.

Don, having taught golf and played competitively for decades, knew this well and could have told me so. Instead he just pointed out a couple of flaws, focusing first on a cupped left wrist, and suggested solutions. In two days, my new swing guru had me on the path to enlightenment. He began to rebuild my broken *Baseball Golf* swing by employing drills selected from a spiral-bound version of the weathered sheets he had sent me. He addressed the flawed areas. He spoke about tempo, torque, release, follow-through, and a sequential approach to building these things into the *Baseball Golf* swing.

Spending a little time with Don left little doubt that his process for creating a golf swing with baseball roots worked. A problem, from my perspective, was that his approach required putting down the clubs and following drills – picking the clubs back up again only after the drills educated body and mind to the nature of the swing. I wanted him to concede and figure out a way to put the clubs into students' hands. My sense was that the larger public, like me, accustomed to a world of instant gratification, would resist giving up the clubs even briefly and even if doing so would make their swing work better.

I also began to see how what Don was doing would work not only for baseball players and natural athletes, but also help the average person to incrementally learn and gain a feeling for what the golf swing is all about.

As I went through the drills, my first thought was that Don was starting with silly stuff. But as I got into them, my first peek into what Don was trying to do encouraged me to look deeper. I began to understand the golf swing by tuning into what my body was feeling – a form of athletic enlightenment. I also began to see how what Don was doing would work not only for baseball players and natural athletes, but also help the average person to incrementally learn and gain a feeling for the golf swing.

From drills on balance, to weight transfer, to turning and coiling, Don's methodology takes you from the ground up to the shoulders, inside your golfer's brain, back out and down – first by hitting balls at knee height, then in gradual stages all the way down to the ground. You'll experience power, confidence, and precision like never before.

Bringing the fresh perspective and new ideas of a writer/student, I worked with Don to make his original drills easier to understand and collaborated on additional drills and imagery.

Still, I urged Don to do something that would allow

students to pick up their clubs as they went through the drills. Steadfast in his conviction, he insisted that a method that works to rebuild golf swings in a way that allows the student not only to swing better, but to understand the swing more clearly.

"It's like the movie *The Karate Kid*. The student wanted to kick, throw punches, and break wood right from the start. Had his teacher allowed that to happen, the only things that would have gotten kicked or broken were the kid's butt and bones," says Don. "Besides, we're not asking them to give up their clubs completely; we want them to go through a simple series of drills to help them develop a great swing."

The drills do not take a lot of time or demand expensive equipment. You can do them in your living room, basement, or garage, on a rainy weekend or when the weather is too cold or too hot to get out and play. Afterword, head for the range or the golf course and approach the game with more confidence.

You're probably wondering if it really works. Besides the endorsements on the outside of this book, I can personally assure you it does. It has helped me develop an understanding of the golf swing that allows me to work on things with a knowledge I never had before. In the past when things went wrong on the golf course I was dumbfounded. *Baseball Golf* has allowed me to identify my own swing flaws and make important corrections, before things get too far out of sync. Remember that 280-yard drive I spoke about earlier? I've had a few more of those and increased my average distance and accuracy off the tee. More recently, I've incorporated te changes into my irons and am scoring better with greater regularity.

– Don Peterson

"The beauty of the Baseball Golf swing is its simplicity. It begins with a swing concept and a basic feeling, then builds on that concept with drills, so you can feel it and play it while improving. Show me a golfer who can't give up the clubs for a couple of days to attain that, and I'll show you a golfer who is doomed to mediocrity at best."

On one magnificent occasion, I hit the ball 295 yards off the tee. It would have gone farther and been my first 300-yard drive at the ripe old age of 57, but, the hole got in the way. Instead it became my first hole-in-one and my first double eagle ever – in one shot!

Lucky? You bet! But you know what they say about luck: it's what happens when you get good (or in my case at least better) at something.

"The beauty of the *Baseball Golf* swing is its simplicity. It begins with a swing concept rooted in a basic feeling and understanding, and then builds on it with a sequence of drills," says Don. "You feel it, you learn it, and you understand it in a way that allows you to swing athletically and with confidence so you can continue to improve. Show me a golfer who can't give up the clubs for a couple of days to attain that, and I'll show you a golfer who is doomed to mediocrity at best."

If you're ready to try the *Baseball Golf* approach and get all that, turn the page. If not, put down this book and be about your game as it currently exists.

– Phil Nero

Chapter 1

Motion 101

WEIGHT TRANSFER AND CENTRIFUGAL FORCE HELP GROOVE AN ATHLETIC SWING

Don Peterson wants you to know three things about *Baseball Golf.*

First, *Baseball Golf* is about adapting a baseball swing for golf.

Second, the process of adapting a baseball swing for golf also incorporates other elements of baseball, especially throwing fundamentals such as a loose grip and using leg muscles to generate ball speed.

Third, and maybe most important, the golf swing is not a vertical swing.

Rather, the golf swing is closely akin to the more horizontal baseball swing, tilted forward to adjust for the ball being a stationary object on the ground.

Perhaps no one ever swung a golf club with greater consistency and precision than the great Ben Hogan, whose swing is probably the most studied and emulated of all time. Baseball Golf can help you achieve the same style of a simple, precise, on-plane swing mastered so magnificently by Mr. Hogan. Top teachers, as well modern golfers such as Nick Faldo, Chad Campbell, and Tiger Woods all use Mr. Hogan's swing as a model.

"Furthermore," says Don, "hitting a ball with a golf club pretty much amounts to throwing the golf club head with precision into the back of the ball. This may explain why baseball pitchers generally have terrific golf swings. As the director of golf at Harbor Club on Lake Oconee, I headed up the annual Atlanta Braves fund-raising tournament. While helping some of the players on the range before a tournament in the mid-1990s, I noticed pitchers John Smoltz, Tom Glavine, and Greg Maddox all possessed very good golf swings, while the better hitters, like Ryan Klesko, Terry Pendleton, and Otis Nixon, all struggled. The reason is simple: the fundamentals of weight transfer for an efficient, athletic golf swing are harmonious with baseball throwing fundamentals."

Baseball Golf is about adapting a baseball swing for golf – it also incorporates other elements of baseball, especially throwing.

Don has observed that other athletes with finely tuned throwing mechanics also possess sound golf swings. Football quarterbacks John Brodie, John Elway, and Tom Brady all have great golf swings. Brodie even competed on the Senior Tour for a while.

ADAPT YOUR BASEBALL SWING FOR GOLF.

GOLF INCORPORATES THROWING FUNDAMENTALS.

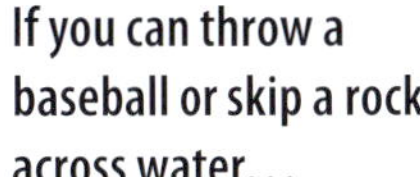

If you can throw a baseball or skip a rock across water...

...you can learn to throw the clubhead with speed and accuracy into the back of a golf ball.

"When you throw a ball, everything you do before releasing it influences ball flight and speed. But once it leaves your hand, you're no longer a factor," says Don. "The same idea applies in golf. Everything you do in your setup, backswing, and downswing influences the way the clubhead flies out and into the ball which, in turn, determines the flight of the ball. But, once the ball leaves the clubface the outcome depends on your swing mechanics – good or bad!"

You will dramatically improve your swing as you work through this book. But first, let's dispel any notion that some quick tip or simple concept can cure what ails your golf swing.

"The movie *Caddyshack* implores us to be the ball. That makes for some great fun in a great film, but it's not reality," says Don. "In reality, we need to imagine what comprises a solid golf swing, then create it. Next we practice it to refine and perfect the desired sequence of motion."

A GOLF SWING IS NOT VERTICAL.

This hand position is too vertical for Don and is probably too vertical for you too.

Baseball hitters keep the bat held high to adjust their swing plane to the ever-changing position of the ball. If the ball were always pitched to the same location, batters could align the bat on the plane of the ball, and hit home runs every time!

The first principle of a proper swing is centrifugal force, a source of energy that requires a circular motion. Somewhere in your academic past you probably had a teacher say something like: "A circle is a closed curve consisting of all points equal in distance from the center."

Similarly, when you swing a golf club, the clubhead traces circular points of equal distance and you – more precisely the center of your body mass – are the center. The better you control this center (located about two inches inside your navel), the more control you have over the path of the clubhead and, subsequently, the ball. However, learning to rotate your torso perfectly around the center of your body mass while you are perched on two legs with intent to strike a golf ball is a tad more difficult than drawing a circle with a compass. For one thing, drawing the circle requires one complete 360° sweep around a fixed point.

The more perfect the rotation of your body or torso, the more repetitive your shot-making can become.

In the case of the compass, the center is defined by a point. If this point does not stray, then the pencil makes a perfect circle.

Similarly, the golfer maintains control over the clubhead, if he or she can control their torso, the golfing equivalent to the center of a circle.

Absorbing the principles of *Baseball Golf* requires some patience. Don't rush to turn pages to find quick answers. Take it drill by drill, chapter by chapter.

In golf, we start at the bottom of the swing, take the club back, coil the torso to create power and energy, and release the clubhead on a forward path. Along the way the clubface meets the ball in a perfect position and continues on a circular path around your center.

Later, Don will introduce steps to perfect your coil creating power for a phenomenal swing. As with any form of enlightenment, absorbing the principles of *Baseball Golf* requires some patience. Don't rush to turn pages to find quick answers. Go drill by drill, chapter by chapter. So, back to the principle at hand – learning to rotate your torso in both an efficient and a repetitive manner.

In the beginning stages of learning to swing, your mind should key on the muscles that control the center of your mass.

To draw the golf swing circle with the clubhead, we must learn to transfer our weight from one leg to the other and then back again. These movements allow us to rotate over the trail hip during the backswing and the lead hip during the follow-through.

Baseball Golf uses a sequence of drills to help your body's kinesthetic powers tap the natural sense of power and comfort you feel in swinging a baseball or softball bat, then morphs these feelings into a powerful, repeatable, golf swing. "*The Baseball Golf Swing Method* will help you develop efficiency in your swing like you've never experienced – just like the effortless swings you admire in many pro golfers," says Don. "Your efforts will be assisted by the methodology a trained physical therapist uses to help patients overcome motion deficiencies and physical injury."

In clinical terms this form of training is known as Propioreceptive Neuromuscular Facilitation (PNF). Its most common use is to help stroke victims regain lost motion and feeling in the arms and legs. PNF relies on repeating a desired motion to reopen damaged nerve channels that run from the muscles directly to the brain. This reconnection between brain and muscles can help the body function properly again. If this system functions well, there will be good body awareness. A weak system may result in clumsiness.

But, you aren't reading this book to learn science and become a physical therapist. You want to become a better golfer with a repeatable, athletic swing, right? Well, believe it or not PNF training can help you get there. "In this instance, PNF can be child's play. Literally," says Don. "Imagine grasping a child by the arms and swinging him or her in a circle around you. When you do that, you are using the resistance of your body's mass to offset the centrifugal pull of the small child outward and away from you. That's basically what you're doing when you swing a golf club."

Try this exercise to learn what centrifugal force should feel like in your golf swing.

Notice the arms of both adult and child are pulled straight, and the little boy is stretched out horizontally at almost a 90° angle to the adult's vertical frame. This outward pull exaggerates the feeling you should strive to develop in your golf swing.

However, a golf club is far lighter than a child. The clubhead weighs only a few ounces. We are challenged to actually feel the weight of the clubhead while whipping it around our bodies at speeds of up to 140 mph and generating in the neighborhood of 2,000 pounds of force at impact. Feeling the clubhead under these circumstances requires trust. You must trust the club just as the child trusts you. So instead of latching onto the club with a tight grip, relax your arms. Relax your grip. Relax your muscles. Allow them the freedom to feel the weight of the clubhead (just a fraction of a child's weight) and trace a circular path from your body's central mass with optimum speed. The *Baseball Golf Swing Method* will help you do just that.

Okay, that takes care of the arms, hands, and torso for the time being. Now, it's time to factor in weight transfer. At the start of this chapter you learned that taking the first step toward building a powerful, repetitive, athletic golf swing requires a general understanding of specific body movements. To begin understanding weight transfer and how to utilize our body's mass in human motion, take a step. That's right, actually stand up and take a step forward.

Before doing so, though, ask yourself: How will I accomplish this motion? What muscles will I use? What causes the step to take place? Don has asked individuals and entire groups of students this question and rarely gotten the correct answer. Most people believe they lift one foot or the other to take a step forward. Many others believe they push off one foot or the other. What actually happens? Find out. Go ahead and take a step.

Unless you're a Dressage horse or some similarly large four-legged mammal prone to prancing, the first thing that actually occurs is a lean. Muscles in the front of your body relax, allowing your body weight to simply start falling forward. After this happens, one foot or the other strides forward to "catch" the weight of your moving mass.

Allow your body mass to start a sequential motion that helps swing the club effortlessly – like a car going downhill.

1 Coast down the hill using only gravity.

2 Drive up the hill with engine.

3 Race down the hill with engine *AND* gravity.

What does all this have to do with the golf swing? Golfers who understand weight transfer, control the center of their body mass, and begin their swing motion from their center have a better chance of controlling where the golf ball eventually lands. If your body performs efficiently, your swing becomes powerful and more repeatable. The body works best when you use your weight, or the momentum of its mass, to push, pull, or lift something – all of which happens to some degree during the swing.

It's time to use your imagination again. This time imagine yourself in a car at the top of a hill. Place the gearshift in neutral, release the brake, and the car begins rolling, gradually gathering speed and momentum as gravity pulls it down the hill.

Now, imagine yourself in the same car at the bottom of the same hill. You have to start the engine and generate force to counteract the pull of gravity to drive the car up the hill. The excessive weight of the car creates a negative pull or drain on the motor as it works to carry the car to the top.

Now make a u-turn and, with the same level of acceleration used to climb the hill, head back down. The power of the engine, coupled with downward force and the pull of gravity, launches you down the hill much faster than you came up. The same amount of power from the engine, coupled with less resistance, generates greater speed.

Applying this imagery and these variables to the golf swing will help you better understand how it should work. If your body mass remains stationary and you begin the backswing with the smaller muscles of the shoulders, arms, and hands, you will place unnecessary strain or pull on these muscles, restricting their power and speed – like a car going downhill with the emergency brake on.

However, if you start your swing with a well-

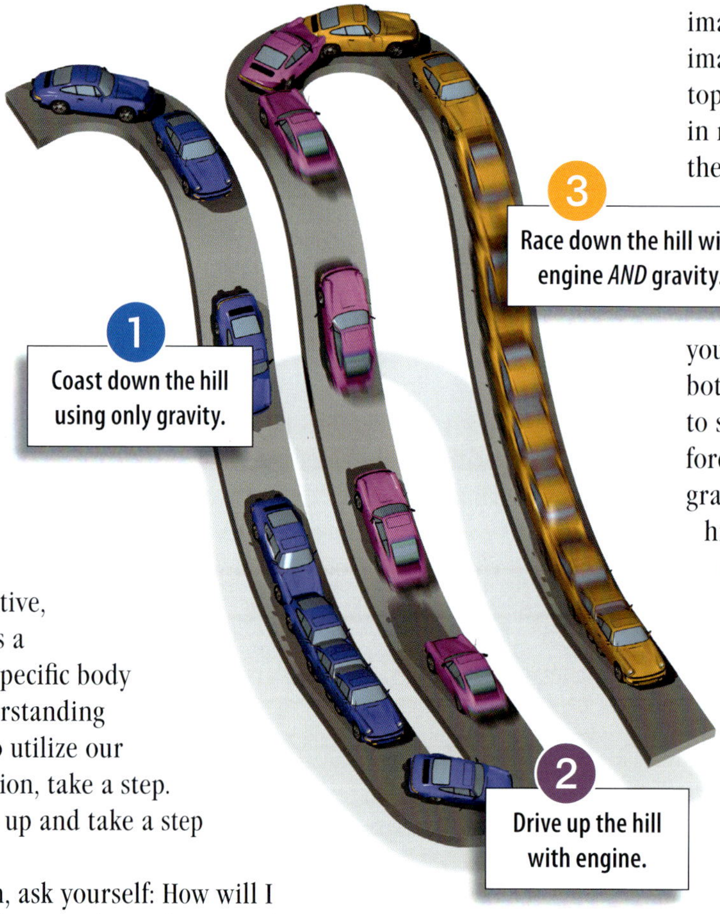

"IN THE WHEELHOUSE"

coordinated, precise weight shift and turn, you allow your body mass to start a sequential motion that helps swing the club effortlessly – like a car accelerating freely downhill.

Before beginning the *Baseball Golf* drill sequence, Don would like to share a few weight transfer and motion thoughts. "Extensive computer analysis indicates that although most golfers' weight may be centered at address, the most efficient downswing starts with a noticeable shift of weight to the lead foot. At the top of their backswing, at least 80% of their weight transfers to the trail foot. By impact they have transferred that 80% back onto their lead foot. Clearly this supports the principle of using your body weight both away from and through toward the target."

That said, it's time to begin your personal journey into *Baseball Golf*. Start by grabbing an iron from your bag. Imagine going back in time to the best "at bat" you ever had in baseball or softball, or a time when you were having fun just playing a game. Close your eyes and visualize yourself back in that place and time. Grip the iron and hold it as if it were a bat. Step up to the plate and swing away.

It's time to start building that same feeling of strength, confidence, and satisfaction into your golf swing. Now let's take it to the golf course. You see, a swing at a baseball in the strike zone is in your "wheelhouse." Problems occur when the ball is down in the dirt, out of your wheelhouse, just where it is all the time in golf.

Baseball Golf will teach you how to adjust your body position, and put the golf ball in your soon-to-be discovered "golf wheelhouse" every time – with an exhilarating feeling of power and athleticism. But to get there, you have to put that iron back in your bag until your body is reprogrammed to use it the right way.

Baseball Golf will teach you how to put the golf ball in your soon-to-be discovered "golf wheelhouse" every time.

The *Baseball Golf* path to proper motion in a golf swing applies to all golfers, regardless of gender or body type. In brief, your mind should key on the muscles that control the center of your mass. Understanding this concept may help you grasp why for years good golfers and instructors have placed so much emphasis on the legs in the golf swing, and why pear-shaped golfers such as Jack Nicklaus, Lee Trevino, Tim

"Lumpy" Herron, and John Daly excel at this sport. Their naturally lower centers of gravity, combined with strong hip and thigh muscles, help them control and power their swings directly from the hips (or core) where, just as in baseball, the swing center is located.

In both sports, the mind's control of body motion relies directly on feedback from your connection with the ground, along with control and balance, to properly use the muscles located in the hips, feet, and legs. Mind and musculature work together to form the golf swing. While some instructors contend that our personalities govern how fast we swing (i.e. fast swingers swing fast because they talk fast, walk fast, and, in general are high-strung. Slow swingers swing slowly because they talk slowly, walk slowly, and are easy-going). The fact is that players can only swing with the speed their individual musculature allows.

"Your arms should swing as fast as your feet, legs, and hips can work together to transfer weight and achieve effective motion," says Don. "Players who learn to allow their arms to swing freely, powered by their lower body's transfer of weight, swing much better than those who do not. Some instructors refer to this concept as matching the upper body to the lower body. Your arms and shoulders should move as a smooth response to the transfer of weight between your feet, legs, hips, and, of course, the center of your body mass. This is where rhythm and tempo originate in the golf swing. That's the secret to a great golf swing."

The importance of this kind of weight transfer in your golf swing cannot be overemphasized.

In a way it's about sound construction, just like the *Three Little Pigs* taught us as kids. A golf swing based on straw or sticks is susceptible to harsh winds the Big Bad Wolf (a.k.a. the Golf gods) can blow its way. *Baseball Golf* is like the house of bricks. It builds your swing on a sound foundation. Then, it completes the process with quality construction materials.

To start building the foundation for a swing that is as solid as a house of bricks, we begin with the simplest of all throwing motions, the underhand toss. Even though you may be skilled at throwing a ball in a variety of ways, going back to your throwing roots will allow you to see how this motion is directly linked to a proper, powerful golf swing.

NOTE: Before beginning the drills in this book it is important to note that they are written using generic language geared for both left- and right-handed players. As you face the ball, the hand, foot, arm, hip, or wrist, etc., closest to the target will be called the *lead*; the hand, foot, arm, hip, or wrist, etc., farthest from the target will be referred to as the *trail*.

DRILL 1 *THE UNDER-HAND THROW* 

From early childhood, our motor skills are developed in stages. Throwing, a motor skill, is no exception. The first time you tossed a ball you probably did so with one arm and with your feet glued to the ground. This worked for those very first short tosses. But to gain power and distance, you progressively moved to higher skill levels. To throw faster and longer underhand tosses you learned to coordinate your arm swing with weight transfer and a short stride. From there you moved all the way up to powerful overhand throws.

The importance of this kind of weight transfer in your golf swing cannot be overemphasized. If you follow the Underhand Throw Drill correctly, you will likely feel the power produced by transferring your weight before you release the ball. Similarly, the transfer of body weight precedes the release in your golf swing and occurs just prior to any turning or coiling of your body. Both your trail leg and your lead leg should take turns supporting your body weight during the swing.

This is an extremely important point in building a strong foundation upon which to construct your golf swing. Here's why: Your trail leg shouldn't bend, bow, or "break down" before any turning or coiling action related to the back swing occurs. Why? For the very same reason baseball pitchers wind up and shift their weight to create power and speed when throwing. In baseball, infielders often encourage pitchers to "rock and fire." When a pitcher rocks, the lead leg comes off the ground and 100% of the body's weight is supported by the trail leg, (which maintains a stable but slightly flexed position) before it is transferred forward, toward the catcher. The pitcher then drives off the back leg toward the plate, propelling the arm and ball toward the target. The ball is launched from the hand at what is referred to as the release point. Proper turning and a consistent release point equal accuracy. (How this relates to the golf swing will be discussed in greater detail later.)

Step and Throw

DRILL 1

THE UNDER-HAND THROW

A Start with your weight leaning slightly on your trail foot (as a softball pitcher would stand with his feet on the rubber). With the ball in your trail hand (about waist high), begin to lean forward **B**. At the same time drop your trail arm allowing it to swing back behind you. **C** Initiate your weight shift by using your lead foot to stride a short step forward to catch the forward transfer of your body weight. As the weight reaches your lead foot, your trail arm should have just reached its peak behind you. If you have allowed your weight to move correctly, you will feel your arm swing forward as your weight continues to transfer onto your lead foot.

As you repeat this motion, pay close attention to how the muscles in your arm swing in harmony with (not independently of) your body as you step forward using the transfer of your body weight to initiate the throw.

SWING NOTE! *Exaggeration can help.*

"In order to feel the motion of a correct swing, it is very important in the beginning stages of training your body to exaggerate movements and make them seem bigger than they need to be. As you progress, you will learn to refine these motions into smaller and more efficient movements," says Don. "I've seen this progression with good players who started very young. It's natural for a child to learn faster and easier.

Put a club in a small child's hands and watch how much he or she uses the body to swing the club. They come by it naturally (out of necessity) because they don't possess the upper body strength to move the club back and forth. As adults we often develop swings lacking in lower body movement because we do possess sufficient upper body strength. By exaggerating and relying on our weight transfer and lower body motions, as children do, we can avoid the problem of swinging only with our upper body."

How you transfer weight to your trail leg is very important. In ❶, Don has shifted his trail leg with a golf club. When the weight of his upper body is placed directly over the club, its shaft remains straight and strong. In ❷, weight and pressure have been applied incorrectly, (angled) causing the club to bend and drastically affect the spine angle.

Learning to correctly place your weight directly over your trail leg will help you avoid two very common swing flaws often developed in the early stages of learning golf that are caused by turning or coiling prior to shifting your weight over your trail leg during the backswing.

Photo ❸ shows an incorrect transfer of weight to the trail leg. This improper shift has caused an outward bow or bend of the trail leg laterally away from the target (often called a sway).

Another common incorrect transfer of weight commonly referred to as a reverse weight shift appears in ❹. A reverse weight shift occurs when the trail leg straightens and the golfers body leans toward the target. Notice in the picture on the far right how the lead knee points out as it absorbs the weight which should be over the trail leg.

Never allow your trail leg to bend, bow, or "break down" throughout the course of your backswing.

NOTICE HOW DRASTICALLY SPINE ANGLE CAN BE AFFECTED BY IMPROPER WEIGHT TRANSFER!

To help you avoid these problems, Don suggests a series of drills to learn the fundamentals of correct weight transfer.

Transfer Weight

DRILL 2

THE MUMMY DRILL

Often in this book you will be asked to use the powers of your imagination to help you feel the correct patterns of movement. The Mummy Drill is a good example of this and will help you learn about weight transfer.

Imagine you are cast in a horror movie, playing the role of an Egyptian mummy bound tightly to your eyeballs and beyond in hundreds of yards of wrappings. You have spent several centuries in a casket and want very much to get out – almost as badly as you want to develop a good, athletic golf swing. Your casket is standing in the corner of a museum, and you want to attract attention by tipping it over. You cannot, of course, move any of your body parts – all that wrapping, remember? Your muscles and joints are locked and rigid.

With your arms across your chest, begin rocking your body back and forth A-B in the hope of tipping over the casket. Feel your weight move from the outside of your left foot to the outside of your right foot. The muscles you are using are the vastus lateralis, the long muscles that run along the outside of your thighs. While practicing this drill you'll probably notice that your head and/or upper torso are swaying back and forth to help you transfer your weight from side to side. This desired outcome is part of the overall transfer of body weight that you need for a successful, efficient swing. In later drills we will modify this rocking motion somewhat by working on rotation. But for now, simply rock back and forth to develop and understand the feel of weight transfer.

Note that your head must move to do the drill correctly. Contrary to what you may have been told, some head movement is necessary in an athletic golf swing (see page 25 for more information on this topic).

If the mummy image strikes you as a bit morbid, there's an alternative image you can use more in keeping with the theme of this book. Pretend instead that you are a rookie baseball player at your first spring training. A few veterans wrap you in trainer's tape and lock you in a free-standing locker. Use the same rocking motion and try to tip the locker, drawing the attention of the equipment manager who will want a chunk of your signing bonus to let you out.

This drill demands more head movement than is required in your golf swing. Don't fear moving your head too much while performing this drill.

Transfer Weight and Pivot

DRILL 3

ROTATION DRILL

This drill emphasizes part of the motion required to properly pivot.

Begin by placing your hands on your stomach **A**, and then lift your lead leg completely off the ground while pointing your lead knee away from the target. This exaggerated motion allows you to feel 100% weight transfer. This 100% transfer is a reference point only, a feeling that will help you later. The actual swinging of a golf club requires about 85% weight transfer. After getting to know what 100% feels like, the pivot can be adjusted accordingly. Put you lead leg back down and do the same thing with your trail knee **B**.

Repeat this over and over until you really get a sense of rotaing and transferring 100% of your weight from leg to leg.

DRILL 4

HIP SLIDE DRILL

This drill is designed to help you initiate the downswing with proper lateral hip movement in only one direction: toward the target!

A Stand with your arms relaxed at your side, feet shoulder-width apart. Without raising your feet off the ground, gently slide your hips away from the target and then back toward the target. Concentrate on the transfer of weight into your trail hip, and then back to your lead hip **B**. Feel your weight transfer into your trail heel, and then back to your lead heel. Your knees will likely lock into a straight position during this drill, causing your weight to flow more to your heels.

Don't worry. You'll learn to keep your legs properly flexed in a later drill. For now, however, we want to combine some of the fundamental motions from Drills 2, 3, and 4 into the next drill.

Practice these drills feeling your weight slide away from the target, then through toward the target. Understand, however, that we only slide toward the target during the actual golf swing.

DRILL 5
THE DANCE DRILL

Now we'll add some rhythm to what we've learned so far.

Do this drill in a 1-2-3 rhythm over and over again. On your turn away from your target (backswing), concentrate on "rolling" your lead heel only slightly off the ground. On your turn to face the target (through-swing), concentrate on allowing your trail foot to come off the ground, all the way onto the tips of your toes.

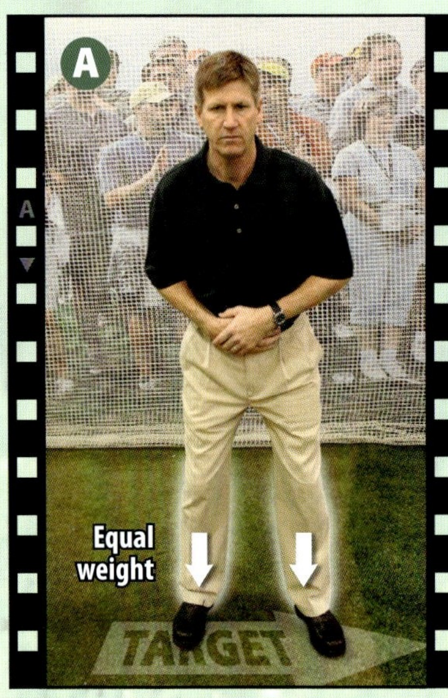

Stand with your legs about shoulder-width apart, your arms folded on your stomach, and, this time, your knees bent slightly.

Begin by turning away from the target about 45° and shift weight onto your trail leg without picking up either foot.

DRILL 5 THE DANCE DRILL ▲

As you go through the motions of this drill, allow your lead foot at least a quarter-turn outward in your address position. This allows for a greater range of motion; you can easily turn your torso to completely face the target on your through-swing. During this particular part of the drill it's okay to turn the lead foot out even farther than a quarter turn to encourage a smoother motion and transfer of weight.

This combination push-off/turn-through motion should result in a finish in which almost all your weight is over the lead foot. The weight of your trail side should come forward to balance over your lead leg and foot. In the follow-through, your back and lead leg should straighten in a natural fashion. Notice how your head moves up to face the target along with the rest of your body, and your trail heel and foot have been pulled up off the ground. This final position should be attained naturally with minimum effort. If you have trouble finishing in a straight, balanced position and facing the target, check the position of your lead foot again. Point it toward the target as much as you have to in order to promote an easy turn through. If necessary, even point it directly at the target.

Remember, you are using both legs, both feet, and the ground to create your turn-through motion. DO NOT use your shoulders to start this motion or you will leave your weight stranded on your trail foot and leg. If you leverage off the ground properly, the motion of your legs, hips, and torso will pull the shoulders around to face the target. Repeat this exercise over and over. Learn to cause this motion without relying on your arms or shoulders.

Think of your upper torso as a bust just sitting on top of your waist waiting to be rotated to and fro.

As you perform these movements, you may think you are learning more about dance than golf. In a sense, you are right. You're learning proper footwork. Think lead heel up (only slightly) and trail heel up all the way onto the tips of the toes. "While practicing this drill, keep your head facing where the ball would be on the turn away from the target, and facing toward the target on the turn through," says Don. "Don't allow yourself to come out of your coil and stand up during your backswing. Do force yourself to

THROUGH-SWING

Slide your hip slightly as you did in the Hip Slide Drill (page 17).

Turn back toward and through to the target until you are facing it straight on.

The Dance Drill using a club.

come out of your coil and stand up tall on your through-swing. I stress the word 'up' because many instructors preach keeping the head down until after the ball is on its way. By studying the swings of great players, you will find this to be incorrect. You'll notice their heads come up immediately as the ball is hit and as the body turns through. In fact, any effort to keep the head down seriously interferes with the body's ability to naturally complete the correct follow-through."

Let your head come up following the clubface as the ball is hit and the body turns through.

Turn... Face the Target

DRILL 6
THE TURN-UP DRILL

Position yourself standing with your lead leg next to a chair or the end of a couch.

Place your arms and hands straight down against the front of your thighs. This helps focus attention on important muscles in the lower body below the waist.

Rock your weight away from the chair as you learned in the Mummy Drill. As your weight rocks back toward the chair, and your lead heel hits the floor...

...turn and bring your trail knee, chest, and torso forward to face the target.

As you rotate to the target, focus on your trail thigh. Be sure your trail thigh comes forward to strike the chair or couch.

To correctly perform this drill, turn your torso a full 90° from start to finish. You should turn your lead foot outward about 45° to promote this full turn.

DRILL 6 *THE TURN-UP DRILL* ▲

This drill teaches you to rely on the muscles of your lower body, especially those in your hips, legs, and feet. "Big muscles of your core and the muscles of your lower body, that's where the golf swing begins, or should," says Don. "That's why I haven't mentioned a thing about the grip yet. Concentrate on the grip first, and you'll have your primary focus forever programmed into your mind's signals to your hands and arms – and you'll always have ball flight problems from slices to hooks, as you struggle in futility to find all the power your inner athlete possesses."

Training with your lead leg next to a barrier (such as a couch or chair) will keep you from sliding your lead hip or lead leg too far toward the target. Your lead knee is

The Turn-Up Drill using a club

forced to straighten, which causes the lead hip to rotate and make room for your trail side to come forward. If you concentrate on bringing your trail knee up to hit the chair or couch, the heel and sole of your trail foot should automatically come completely off the ground, up onto the tip of your big toe.

Keep the shoulders passive during these drills, as you should try to keep them passive during your swing. In other words, relax the shoulders. Tension in the shoulder area is Public Enemy No. 1 of an athletic golf swing. Focus on the motions involved in bringing the trail knee forward along with standing up tall, straightening the lead leg as you turn to face your target.

While concentrating on this motion, feel your weight transfer from your trail foot immediately to your lead foot at the same time your stomach and hip muscles rotate your torso to face the target.

Once you have established an efficient weight transfer, concentrate on straightening your lead leg as you follow through. Feel as if you are standing up as you turn through. In reality, you are. The backswing is a coiling motion, and the follow-through is a releasing motion. Make sure that during your through-swing you release your body up into a finished position in which you not only feel tall, but stand tall.

To gain maximum benefit from this drill, remember that you must not take a backswing as you practice.

Finish tall, comfortable, and balanced.

GET ADDITIONAL FEEDBACK

"Try practicing this drill with your cleats on and preferably on a coarse strain of grass such as Bermuda or Zoysia," says Don. "Wearing cleats will enable you to 'listen' for feedback. If you don't shift your weight smoothly before driving your trail knee forward, you'll hear your spikes tear grass as your trail foot spins in place.

If done correctly, your lead foot remains in position to support proper weight transfer to your lead side, and your spikes will not make noise. Your turn-through should be brisk but quiet. Take your practice outside and listen to see if your trail foot is quiet or noisy."

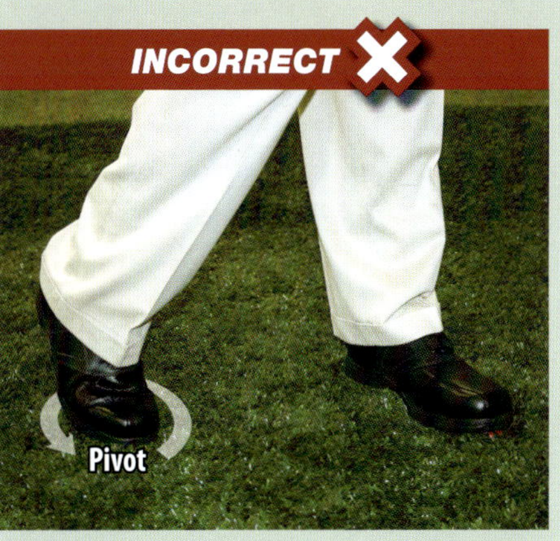

Fine-tune Your Footwork

DRILL 7

THE TOE DRAG DRILL

The Toe Drag Drill helps modify your baseball swing for golf, especially with regard to finishing in a balanced forward position.

To help ensure you achieve the proper motion to finish well, drag your trail toe forward as you complete the Turn-Up Drill. This exaggerated effort is especially helpful in ensuring a proper, tall finish, all the way up onto the tips of the toes of the trail foot.

"This is just a practice drill and should not be used when you actually begin hitting," says Don. "It helps you experience what a proper finish feels like. I'll use this drill occasionally with some of my most stubborn and stationary students. The toe drag may remind you of characteristics of Greg Norman's swing. Not a bad motion to emulate."

DRILL 8

THE LEAD HEEL DRILL

Isolate and feel the proper motion of the lead heel by practicing these movements both correctly and incorrectly in front of a mirror.

When you coil correctly from the center of your body mass, your lead heel will roll in. If you improperly use your shoulders, the lead heel may turn out. If your heel turns out, correct it now. This minor flaw can lead to major problems. Concentrate on the movement of your lead hip. The lead hip and knee should drag the lead heel toward the trail foot as shown. If problems persist, read the next chapter on balance and then return to this drill. Sometimes this problem will disappear only after a student's balance has been corrected.

"Performing this drill in front of a mirror both correctly and incorrectly allows your mind and body to feel the differences. Your lead knee should always feel relaxed, even passive," says Don. "If you feel any form of tension or sense of weight falling onto the lead knee, continue to experiment until you attain a comfortable position and the lead ankle rolls in properly. When you feel the correct motion, practice it again and again."

CORRECT

INCORRECT

Don't worry about head movement. Some head movement encourages the good weight transfer and motion essential to an athletic swing. The head should move about two inches away from the target to help load body weight over the trail hip.

To earn credits in Don's Motion 101 Class, remember the following important points. "Many students," he says, "restrict their motion and weight transfer during these drills out of fear of swaying or moving their heads. Chances are the first piece of advice some of you received was, 'Don't move your head!' It may sound like a valid golf mantra, but it induces a step down the wrong path to swing enlightenment. No matter what you've been told before, don't worry too much about head movement. More problems are caused by a lack of motion as opposed to too much motion. Trying to keep your head in the same position throughout your swing can be a detriment to the good weight transfer and motion essential to an athletic golf swing."

Remember, your head is not your swing's center, your core is. Your head should actually move an average of about two inches away from the target during the backswing. This head movement promotes the desired weight transfer onto a stable trail hip and encourages proper rotation of the torso around the core. It is more important to maintain a stable trail hip than a still head. The head serves only as a tool with which to see, think, and correctly execute these essential motions."

Don has this advice, "Let go of your fears – not only in these drills but later as you swing the club and strike the ball. Let go of your fears about swaying or moving your head. Keep an open mind as you read this book. Practicing the concepts in these drills and applying them to your swing, will help you develop a more reliable and repeatable swing."

Chapter 2

Catch Your Balance

GOOD BALANCE MAKES FOR GOOD GOLF

There are many major enemies of a sound athletic golf swing, but none ranks higher than lack of balance. Balance is the foundation upon which all else is constructed. You've probably heard the term "swing from the ground up." Well, you don't need a sports psychologist to tell you that if you're unbalanced and not well-grounded, this game will drive you crazy. Simply put, good balance leads to better control of your body and your game.

"If asked to name a sport that requires great balance, most people would probably think of the balance beam and put Olympic gymnasts at the top of their lists," says Don. "The way gymnasts maneuver their bodies in mid-air, spin, twist, and are still able to consistently stick their landings demands precision."

You may not think the golf swing is as athletic as these gymnastic maneuvers, but similar levels of balance and control are required when you are coiling and uncoiling during your golf swing. Balance and control can help you create a nearly perfect circle and efficient centrifugal motion. Tapping into a good baseball image will help you even more as you work to build familiar athletic motions into a solid, balanced golf swing.

Consider Hideki Matsui of the New York Yankees and the wonderful balance he demonstrates when swinging a baseball bat. Matsui grooved his swing through years of discipline and training in Japan. He produces consistently here in the U.S. hitting with power and for average while driving in more than 100 runs every year.

Matsui stands evenly balanced, feet parallel, relaxed at the knees. If he were to tilt forward slightly at the hips and drop his bat into a golf address position, you would see an almost perfect golf set-up. Matsui is able to transfer his weight from side to side, coil his body, and make consistent, powerful contact because his balance keeps him poised and ready for just about any pitch. Rarely do opposing pitchers fool him badly or strike him out.

Good balance leads to better control of your body and your game...

... in both baseball and golf.

"One of the most common faults of beginning golfers is their tendency to lean too far forward to reach the ball. This causes their weight to fall forward onto the toes or balls of their feet which can be problematic in both baseball and golf," says Don. "Before moving into the intricacies of motion and weight transfer, you need to learn about correct balance."

When setting up for your swing, you may find yourself out of balance or off center if you:

1. Lean too far forward on the balls of your feet or toes
2. Lean too far back on your heels
3. Lean away from the target
4. Lean toward the target

If you stand in any of these out-of-balance positions, the muscles of your legs will become tight. To experience this for yourself, find your center by standing erect and balanced. Lean forward. Feel the weight of your mass move toward the balls of your feet. Feel the muscle tighten that run from the tips of your toes up your shins to your knee caps. With club in hand, you may feel even greater tightness, extending farther up your legs to the middle of your thighs.

"Leaning forward is the most common off-center fault in golf because we lean over to address the ball," says Don. "Some people, however, set up in other unbalanced positions, often because of some instructional article they've read or video they've seen. Efficient motion needs to be defined. The start of your swing is critical in learning to swing effortlessly. We know muscles and joints move most efficiently when they are in balance and relaxed."

Consider again the example of a car traveling uphill vs. downhill. You can easily understand how pre-setting weight in any direction inhibits the momentum that can be used to your advantage in the beginning stages of an efficient swing.

Continue experimenting by leaning back so your weight falls on your heels. Then, lean right and then left – again feeling the stress which leaning in any direction puts on the muscles of your feet and legs.

Now lean forward again onto the balls of your feet. Feel the stress this places on the muscles of your abdomen. "This forward lean can be especially detrimental because it gives the muscles in your abdomen and legs a job to do, the wrong job!" says Don. "They are busy trying to keep you from falling down. These muscles should be free to rotate your torso during your golf swing!"

Putting yourself in a totally balanced position allows your mind and body to work together to maintain your balance so the important muscles of your lower body and abdomen can remain relaxed and free to properly initiate your golf swing. Let's try some drills to reinforce this concept.

DRILL 9 BALANCE BY THE BUCKETSFULL

"When I was a kid growing up on a farm in Illinois, I used to carry large buckets of feed and water to the livestock every day. This helped me learn how to distribute the work load evenly onto my feet and throughout my body. I didn't know it then, but it was helping my golf swing. It can help yours too."

"By learning to set up in balance, you can eliminate the disastrous effects of starting in an out-of-balance position. Picture a tightrope walker in a circus. The mind constantly alters the body's equilibrium to maintain balance on the wire." says Don. "The same thing would apply to golfers who set up out of balance on purpose or accidentally. As soon as they begin their swing, the vestibular sensors in the ears instinctively make corrections and pull them back

Find Your Balance

DRILL 9

BALANCE BY THE BUCKETSFULL

Hold two pails of water, one in each hand. The extra weight will make it necessary to stand with your back straight and body in perfect balance.

Hold your head up naturally without bending or leaning in any direction. Feel where the weight of your body falls on your feet; try to determine where your weight is when you stand naturally. Through the function of the vestibular sensors in your ears, your mind will tell you when your weight is distributed equally and you are in balance. When you find yourself in a balanced position, remember what it feels like. Then transfer this feel into your golf posture, setup, and swing.

Warning: Beginning your swing out of balance engages the mind in all kinds of corrective counter balancing activity that inhibits good golf swing fundamentals.

into balance. This involuntary correction causes the arc of the swing to be affected unpredictably, making it highly improbable that the clubhead could ever return to the ball correctly."

Another image that helps you start off in a balanced position is a table. A table has four legs and four points of contact with the ground. While we balance ourselves on two legs in golf, we would be wise to consider we do so on four points, just like a table. "I don't want to keep dismissing that *Caddyshack* concept of being the ball. But being the table, at least where your setup is concerned, makes a whole lot more sense," says Don. You can feel what it's like to be as stable as a table, or at least distribute your weight on four points of balance like a table does, by using something other parts of your body normally take comfort in – a pillow.

Stable as a table!

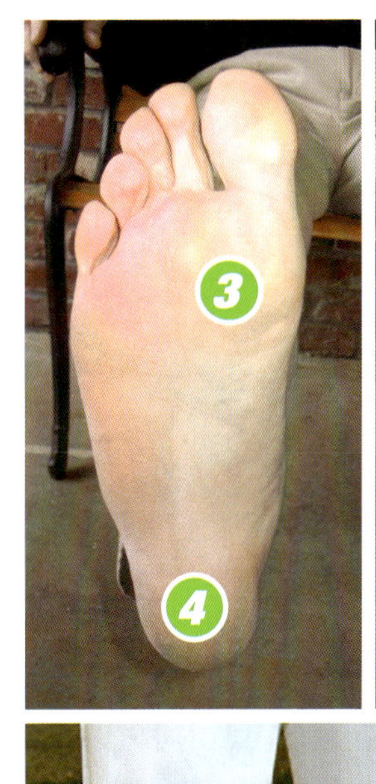

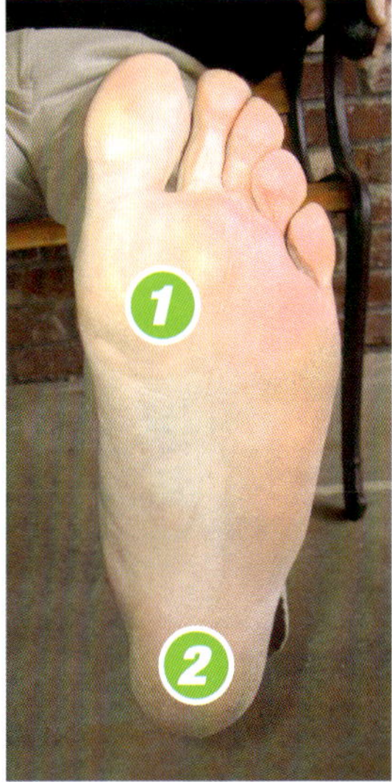

DRILL 10 THE PILLOW DRILL ▼

Now that you understand four points of balance are better than two, you need to learn to feel points of balance on the bottoms of your feet. The great Sam Snead used to take off his shoes and play barefoot when he lost the precision of his game. He did this because he knew being even slightly off balance changes the swing arc. Playing barefoot helped him connect with the points of balance where the feet meet the ground. You can feel these with the help of a pillow or cushion.

Test Your Balance

DRILL 10

THE PILLOW DRILL

While most pillows will work for best results, use a foam-filled sofa cushion. If a single large cushion isn't available, two smaller pillows will also work.

Stand on the cushion and assume your normal golf address position. Notice how any leaning (forward or backward, to the left or right) is exaggerated while standing on the pillow and may cause you to lose your balance and fall in whichever direction you tend to lean.

After you have mastered simply balancing your body on the pillow, try adding some motion by executing your backswing and through-swing.

On toes

Balanced

On heels

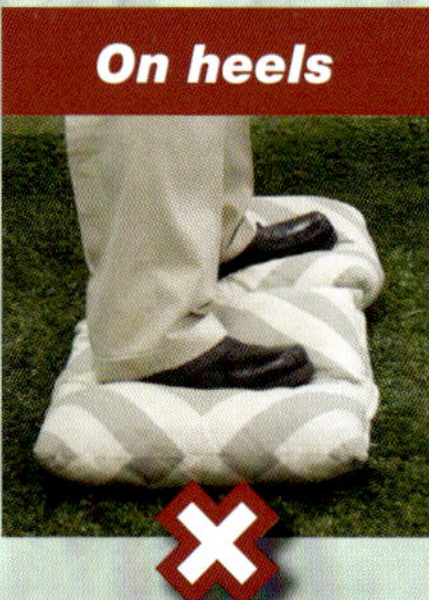

When you can rotate correctly on a pillow and still maintain your balance, you are ready to move on. Later, try combining this drill with the 5-iron drill described in the next chapter.

DRILL 11 TAKING THE PROPER STANCE

Another key component in maintaining balance throughout the golf swing is determining how far apart to place your feet. Most good instructors can adjust a student's stance by looking at the physical characteristics of the student, the length of the club in hand, and the shape of their golf swing. Clearly, Don can't offer a personal visit with every book, but he can help you find the stance width your own subconscious knows is best for you, one you can adjust and build on as you progress in confidence, skill, and stability.

"In the beginning stages of building a better *Baseball Golf* swing, I prefer a narrow stance to promote correct and efficient weight transfer. Only after you have mastered the art of shifting your weight does it make sense to widen your stance, and then only with the longer clubs," says Don. "Unfortunately you probably don't know what is considered narrow or wide for you. But I have a little trick that allows you to consult your own body on how far apart you should place your feet for your best golf swing."

Everyone has a comfortable gait or length of stride when they walk. In his many years of advising thousands of students, Don discovered that the length of one's stride while placing one foot in front of the other is a great way to measure the best position from which to comfortably manage a balanced, efficient transfer of weight.

Check Your Width

DRILL 11

TAKING THE PROPER STANCE

The proper width of your stance can be determined by the length of your stride.

A Wet the bottoms of your feet and walk normally across a stretch of sidewalk or concrete driveway. **B** With tape or chalk immediately mark the distance between the prints before they dry out. Mark the inside distance, toe to heel. Take your stance by placing both feet parallel to the two marks.

C Line up the inside of your lead foot on one mark and the inside of your trail foot on the other. This identifies the correct width for your driver stance – or the widest your feet should be for any normal, full golf swing.

"Placing your feet wider than this could inhibit your ability to transfer weight from one foot to the other, while placing your feet closely together can still produce a stable base," cautions Don. "So, I prefer that you adjust your stance proportionately as you improve your ball-striking ability and use different clubs."

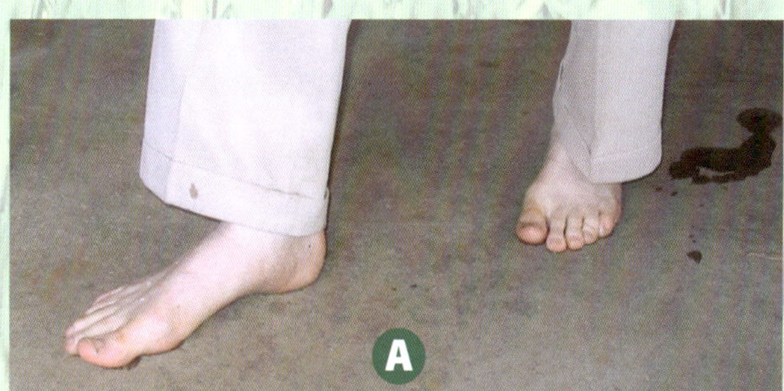

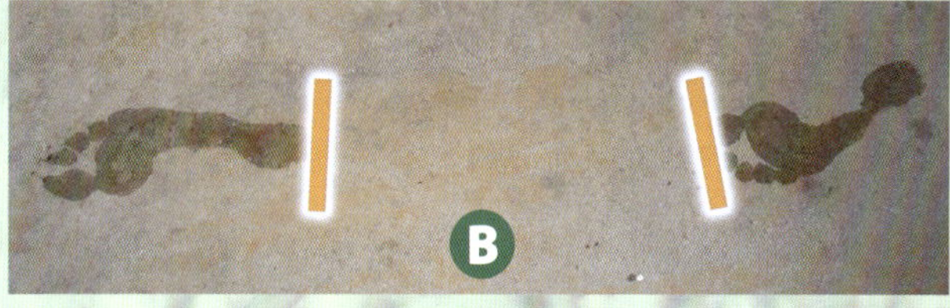

After completing the drills in this book, experiment within these boundaries to make adjustments in the width of your stance for each club chosen. Your stance is widest with your driver and becomes slightly more narrow as each club shortens.

Chapter 3

Be the Pen and the Rubber Band

RELAX YOUR ARMS TO SPEED UP YOUR SWING

Having learned to distribute your weight properly and to stand in balance, you need a posture that is appropriate for golf. In a model golf swing, it is easy to see that the club swings most efficiently and centrifugally at a 90° angle to its axis which is your torso. Once you establish this angle in your address position, you are also establishing the plane on which you should swing the club.

"Your torso is your center. Feeling your center and knowing what happens at your center is important because it affects every part of your golf swing," says Don.

In a system of circular motion, most people incorrectly pay attention to what is happening on the perimeter of the circle as opposed to what is happening at the center. Consider a carousel, for example. The most noticeable horses are in the outside row. They move much faster than the row closest in toward the driveshaft, which is at the very center of the carousel and hardly appears to be moving at all. Even though the drive shaft and the outside horses move at different speeds, their revolutions per minute (rpms) are equal.

The movement of the driveshaft may appear slow compared to the outside horses, but the importance of this core motion is totally essential to (and responsible for) everything happening on the perimeter.

"Similarly, students trying to learn the golf swing, and many teachers as well, pay too much attention to what the arms, hands, and the club are doing as they swing around the outside of the circle," says Don. "The motion in the interior core of a golf swing goes virtually unnoticed and unpracticed, although, as with the carousel, it's largely responsible for all that happens on the perimeter of the circle."

Just as the driveshaft is the source of the carousel's power and motion, the source of power and motion of the golf swing should be created at the center by your torso, hips, and legs. The movements do not need to be extraordinary. They need to be efficient and precise. The objective is to turn correctly, coil efficiently, and create torque. The best way to accomplish this is to keep your movements short and controlled.

Ben Hogan spoke of a breakthrough in his understanding of the golf swing and how it works when he pictured his swing on an inclined plane. While in the address position, he described a pane of glass resting on his shoulders with a hole big enough for his head to stick

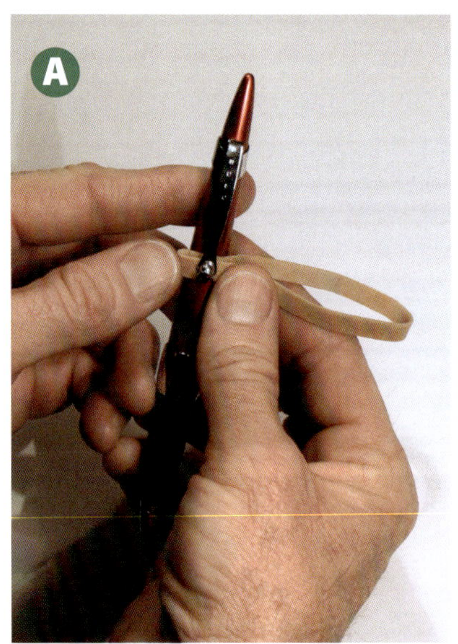

through. The glass slanted on an angle, extending from his shoulders to a point even with the ball and resting on the ground. He believed golfers should strive to swing their arms and club back and forth under the glass on both the backswing and through swing.

That image of a pane of glass, while geometrically sound, is complicated and encourages rigidity in the golf swing. Who can relax and be loose while swinging a club around a pane of glass?

Don prefers a different image to help students envision how a golf club should swing around the body on an imaginary plane. It is a simple analogy that is ingenious because a three dimensional model of the image can be easily constructed, held, and observed. This image also promotes an understanding of highly desirable swing traits great golfers possess and so many teachers strive to impart with disappointing success.

The analogy promotes proper posture and a loose grip. It helps, as Sam Snead says, make the golf swing "greasy, real greasy." And, it also conjures up a great *Caddyshack*-like image of its own. What Don wants you to do is "Be the pen and the rubber band."

It's easy to construct this hands-on visual model that demonstrates swing plane, centrifugal force, and how you should posture your body to produce the desired angles in your golf swing. It leaves you with an image that will help you with so many other key elements crucial to an efficient, powerful golf swing.

Slip a rubber band under the pocket clip of a typical, inexpensive ballpoint pen. Hold the pen between your thumbs and forefingers at about a 45° angle. Twirl it back and forth in place and observe the whip-like action of the rubber band. As the shaft of the pen turns, it serves as an axis for the free-flying rubber band, which swings at a 90° angle to the pen.

Observe how the rubber band lags behind the motion of the pen's axis – just as the club lags in a powerful, athletic golf swing. Observe also how the pen turns, just as the torso should, and how it coils and powers the whip-like motion of the rubber band. The same action is seen in great golf swings when the arms swing freely around the torso.

To more clearly understand this pen and rubber band analogy, hold a pen diagonally over the photo below. Align the pen over the golfer's spine angle. Now twirl the pen back and forth to simulate this same winding and unwinding of a professional golfer's torso. This demonstrates the importance of forming specific posture and swing angles in your swing. It also demonstrates the importance of relaxing your arm muscles and maintaining a light grip to maximize clubhead speed. This will be discussed in greater detail later.

You can tell a high handicapper from a low handicapper and evaluate most golfers by focusing solely on the downswing. A shaft aligning with the trail forearm most often results in a low handicap, while a more vertical position results in a high handicap.

While you may be able to tell high handicappers from the pros by looking at their downswing plane, it is more difficult when looking at their backswing plane. Look at these different swing patterns comparing them to a plane angle established by the club shaft in the address position.

❶ shows a club being swung to the lower side of the shaft plane angle. Golfers in the know call this swinging "inside". Most teachers agree that this position in poorer playing students often

BACKSWING

leads to an off-plane downswing. However, there are professionals who swing inside during the backswing but return to impact coming *on*-plane with a "loop" in their swing. Raymond Floyd and Nancy Lopez have done quite well swinging this way. On the other end of the spectrum you have players like Jim Furyk and Lee Trevino who take the club away from the ball "outside" or higher than the plane of the club shaft they establish at address ❷, then loop the club back on-plane as they start down toward the ball as shown in ❻. It can be difficult for a teacher to decipher how a student may best learn to swing "on-plane" to deliver a square clubface to the ball at impact. Many teachers work solely on students' backswings to help them "find the slot" for an on-plane downswing, while another teacher may work more diligently with a player on his downswing and impact positions to achieve positive results. But a good teacher can do both. You as a student may also improve by understanding these preferences. Continue studying ❹ and ❺ which illustrate poor downswing patterns. ❹ shows how a clubhead may come too inside-out (or under) the shaft path, and ❺ shows again how a clubhead may swing into the ball from outside-in, or over the shaft plane. The goal of *Baseball Golf* is to teach you to learn the feel of a swing that is "on-plane" going back and "on-plane" coming down – or as close to this ideal as possible. Having learned to be the pen by correctly executing the drills to this point in the book, your arms, wrists and hands need only to relax to grip the club in becoming the rubber band.

Our goal in baseball golf is to teach you to learn the feel of a swing that is on-plane going back and on-plane coming down… or as close to this ideal as possible.

DOWNSWING

Many great golfers and instructors (Sam Snead, Ben Hogan, Harvey Pennick, Jack Nicklaus, Tom Watson to name a few) tell you to relax the grip and arm muscles. Such knowledgeable golfers believe that a tight grip and tense muscles are swing enemies. If you think of your arms as rubber bands and your coiled torso as the pen, you must allow your arms and grip to relax.

How can your arms be whip-like if the muscles are rigid and the grip tight? With arms gently "clipped" in place but hanging loosely, they are free to wrap around the coiled body and release like the rubber band. With the hands loosely gripping the club, it is free to act like a rubber band, with speed (which equals power) at the tip (the clubhead).

Grip tightly at the juncture of the hands and the club, and you retard the motion and speed of the club. Arms and club together are the rubber band. Your torso is the pen. Be the pen and the rubber band!

It is impossible to be the pen and the rubber band if you have too much pressure in your hands and/or too much tension in your muscles. So be the pen and the rubber band.

Does this sound repetitive? Good! It cannot be repeated enough.

Grip and muscle tension aside, the effectiveness with which you can allow yourself to be the pen and the rubber band is intimately related to proper posture and clearance around the body. The posture you use is unique to your body size and build. Shorter people will usually stand taller, with less flex or bend in their stance. Taller people, in contrast, will have to *scrunch* their bodies by flexing at the knees, tilting more than may feel comfortable.

DRILL 12 THE CLEARANCE DRILL ▼

Drills 12 and 13 will help you create the angles and posture that permit the arms to swing freely around your torso.

"Allowing your arms to hang in front of you creates what I call clearance," says Don. "This is the area between your upper thighs and your hands when your arms are hanging comfortably in front of you. The amount of space between hands and thighs may vary among students, but generally measures in the neighborhood of about four or five inches. Many students don't allow their arms to actually hang; instead, they hold their arms out as if pointing to the ball."

To position your arms correctly, let them dangle (like rubber bands). When you allow your arms to dangle, relaxation spreads throughout the entire upper body – this also provides you with an accurate assessment of proper clearance.

Allow Clearance

DRILL 12
THE CLEARANCE DRILL

You will need to use a mirror to check your posture or trust the eye of a friend.

Ⓐ Begin by standing up straight, feet shoulder width apart, weight evenly distributed, chin up and chest out. Bending only at the hip joints, push your buttocks backwards as if you were bumping someone off the dance floor! If you have trouble with this, try holding a club or broomstick horizontally just under your pelvic bone and push backward on it. Keep you chin up and chest out.

Ⓑ To experience the correct position of your arms in a "dangling" position, just lower the broomstick down in front of you and hold it loosely. Now flex your knees slightly. You should feel your weight in exactly the same balanced position as when you were standing erect.

"Most students struggle to create clearance between their hands and thighs. You may need to exaggerate this stance by pushing your seat out to develop the proper clearance position," advises Don.

"Sticking your seat out in this exaggerated fashion will also serve as counterbalance to the weight of your head, shoulders, arms, and hands – all of which are leaning forward, creating a 'tilt' in your torso as you face the ball. I encourage you to stand in front of a mirror to practice this posture. You may feel like you are in a rather silly position when you assume this greatly exaggerated posture. Some of my students even tell me it feels obscene! Don't worry. It feels stranger than it looks and will only encourage correct posture. Initially this posture may also cause discomfort in your lower back – a common occurrence that should diminish with practice."

TO ACHIEVE THE PROPER POSTURE...

...EXAGGERATE!

Practice perfect posture holding a 5-iron. Then try switching between your longest club (the driver) and your shortest club (your sand wedge).

Your stance should *feel* exactly the same with all clubs. The ball position will simply change to accommodate the different shaft lengths.

Straighten Your Spine

DRILL 13

THE 5-IRON DRILL

Use this drill to grasp the feeling of keeping your spine (axis) straight and your chin up.

Hold your 5-iron by the clubhead in your trail hand. Lift the shaft over your shoulder and extend it down your spine. Simultaneously, touch the grip end of the club to your tailbone and the shaft (held in your trail hand) to the back of your head.

While keeping your tailbone and your head both touching the shaft, bend forward and slightly flex your knees.

Maintain the spine angle and bent position while dropping your arms and allowing them to dangle freely and relaxed. Your back is straight, your arms are hanging, and your clu shaft is 90° in relation to your spine.

SWING **NOTE!** *One size almost fits all.*

Club fitting and the length of your clubs are also factors. A person's posture is determined by the proportions of his or her body and the length of the club in hand. Most people believe that the length of a golfer's clubs should be decided by the height and proportions of the person swinging them. This is not quite true. The length of a golf club is primarily determined by the length and width of standard golf courses. If it were not for the design of modern golf courses (mainly the narrow fairway landing areas) taller players would be able to use longer clubs proportionate to their height, and their swings would appear more like those of average-size golfers.

But a problem occurs when length is added to a golf clubs: the longer the club, the more flexible and heavier it becomes. When you reach a certain point (about 45 or 46 inches), longer shafts become impractical on a standard golf course. It becomes nearly impossible to swing the club, not only because of the extreme weight, but also because a lack of control causes shots to be more erratic. Slices and hooks stray farther off line and may not stay on the course. Therefore, all golfers, whether they're 5'11" or 6'11", end up playing clubs of similar lengths.

Conversely, shorter people shouldn't choose shorter clubs. That would reduce the width and length of their golf swing arcs, which are already diminished by their physical make-up. Instead they should opt for longer clubs (if they possess the required strength to swing them), increase their arc and clubhead speed and keep up with their taller, larger opponents.

This is why it appears that many women on the LPGA Tour have longer clubs, especially their lofted woods. Shorter in stature, their clubs appear longer.

Without changing your spine angle or the flex in your knees, grip the club normally and let the clubhead rest on the ground.

Your clearance posture is now correct.

Keep in mind, too, that while feeling about the same, your posture doesn't actually stay the same for every club. The club length and terrain both figure into posture adjustments. Don suggests an exaggerated image to make this point. Picture two golfers, one holding a 10-foot club ❶ and the other a three-foot club ❷. The golfer with the 10-foot club has to stand much farther away from the ball – spine angle, chest, and eyes all making adjustments at address, with the ball somewhere around 12 feet away.

This position is radically different from the golfer with the shorter club who stands much closer to the ball at address with spine, chest, and eyes angled sharply down at the ball sitting very close below. This exaggeration makes it easy to understand that while we make every effort to set up in a similar posture for every shot, we must adjust according to the situation. Club length and whether the ball is sitting below or above your feet are the most common variables. Gripping down on a club, or bending slightly more or less at the hips are the most common adjustments.

But for any of these angles and positions to work properly, you must be the pen and the rubber band. And in order to be the pen and the rubber band, you must also learn to wind and uncoil your body. You are simulating this motion when you spin the pen in your fingers. Again, the pen is your torso and the rubber band your arms working bilaterally as one unit (remember swinging the child).

"The first step is the coiling action. You'll recall that in Drill 6 we discussed how to be balanced and feel your center. The object is to turn correctly, coil efficiently, and create torque. In golf, the best way to accomplish this is to keep your movements short and controlled, not long and uncontrolled. Let's learn how.

Although setting up with a 10-foot or a 3-foot club would *feel* nearly the same, your posture doesn't actually stay the same.

Chapter 4

The Windup

USING THE CLUBHEAD TO THROW STRIKES AT THE BALL

In this chapter you will draw on the skills you developed in your youth to throw a baseball with power and accuracy and apply these familiar skills as part of a powerful, athletic golf swing. If you never played baseball or softball, or weren't much of a thrower, don't worry. We've added drills in this chapter to train your body to perfect the windup needed for your golf swing.

Picture a big league pitcher going into his wind-up. All the weight leaves his lead leg as he lifts his lead knee up. No experienced pitcher would ever try to throw a pitch without making this motion which results in a transfer of weight to the trail leg. The speed and power with which a pitch is unleashed comes from this initial weight transfer and the subsequent driving forward off the trail foot to deliver the pitch. The golf swing employs the same principle.

To understand this more clearly, take a normal windup and throw a ball as hard as you can. You can use any kind of ball, even a small rubberized ball like a tennis ball. Find a place where you can actually throw it as hard as you can. Feel how you use your legs to throw the ball.

Now, try throwing a ball as hard as you can without picking up your lead foot – more or less flat footed. Feel the lack of power when trying to throw the ball without shifting your weight to the trail leg!

Yet, it is common among poor golfers to maintain far too much weight on the lead foot as they wind and coil their bodies to throw the clubhead and strike the ball. It even has a name in the golf world – the reverse pivot or the reverse weight shift. The drills in this chapter are designed to help you learn proper weight transfer while coiling into your trail leg. This combination of lower body motions comprise what is arguably the single most important ingredient to converting a poor or weak golf swing into a sound and powerful one.

The speed and power with which a pitch is unleashed comes from this initial weight transfer – the golf swing employs the same principle.

Whether you're learning these motions for the first time or adapting them from previously learned throwing motions, weight transfer helps create additional power and clubhead speed as you step into and turn through a golf ball during your golf swing.

"One of my Japanese students once said something to me that will help you understand how correct weight transfer feels. Often when I teach weight transfer, students focus on where to place the weight. The weight shifts to the trail foot during the backswing, then back onto the lead foot on the through-swing. This particular Japanese student helped himself. He exclaimed 'Ah, very light!' He was referring to the sensation he had in his lead foot. Rather than feeling the transfer of weight move onto his trail foot, he instead felt the weight move *off* his lead foot. Clearly, if the goal is to transfer weight to the trail foot, then certainly you must feel weight come off the lead side, making it feel 'very light!'"

Feel the Flex

DRILL 14

THE HEAVY WEIGHT DRILL

This drill will help you learn to stabilize your trail knee.

Start this drill from the clearance posture we learned in Chapter 3. If you don't own a medicine ball, substitute a bowling ball or a shag bag full of golf balls.

A With knees flexed, hold your arms out, elbows tucked into your midsection, and palms facing upward underneath the heavy weight.

Keeping the weighted object directly in front of you, turn away from your target **B** as if winding up to throw the object as far toward the target as you are physically capable.

While turning away, try to keep your weight on the inside of your trail foot to maintain balance and control of the heavy weight. You may want to pre-set your weight toward the inside of your trail foot.

Essentially, this student created a verbal cue to help him properly repeat a very important muscle movement. It is of utmost importance to understand that anyone who has ever swung a golf club, even once, has programmed a particular sequence of muscle movements into the brain. (See the Swing Note below.)

DRILL 14 THE HEAVY WEIGHT DRILL ▲

The Heavy Weight Drill is a core exercise that will teach you to keep your trail hip and leg flexed as you practice your backswing. This drill specifically defines the desired motion for hitting a golf ball. By coiling the big muscles of the torso and legs as you turn away from your target, you can use them to swiftly pull a weighted object, such as a clubhead, in rotation toward the target in an uncoiling motion.

SWING NOTE! *Verbal cues help program your swing.*

"Problems occur when the mind/muscle programming initiates muscle movements that result in bad shots," says Don. "Unfortunately, getting rid of incorrect programming is not easy. While working through the next series of drills, you will more than likely find yourself using different muscle movements than those used in your old swing."

To keep from using old programming and incorrect muscles, use verbal cues (just as Don's Japanese student did) to create and install a new program in your brain to help you initiate correct muscle movement sequences.

"Much of my success in teaching comes from my use of verbal cues during instructional sessions. I experiment with different words until one clicks with each student, triggering certain movements and establishing a correct, new mind/muscle movement pattern or program," says Don. "I encourage you to say out loud the verbal cues supplied with many of the drills that follow. Your swing will be the better for it."

The Heavy Weight Drill and subsequent drills in this chapter will help train your body to wind and coil properly.

While working through the Heavy Weight Drill, pay close attention to your trail knee and trail hip. Your trail knee should be flexed slightly in the address position and remain flexed throughout the coiling motion involved in your backswing.

The trail hip should also feel flexed. It may feel as if you are squatting and moving your hip downward as you coil away from the target. This is how it should be. If the trail knee is to remain in the desired flexed position throughout the coiling motion, your trail hip (as well as your entire torso) must lower ever so slightly.

"I call this 'sitting into the trail hip'," says Don. In the beginning, exaggerate the squat to keep your trail knee flexed. Repeat the verbal cue "sit" out loud every time you practice this motion.

Try to keep the lead knee pointed in as you turn away from the target. Incorporate the feeling of sitting down with these keys and you will create a tremendous amount of torque in your legs and hips during the backswing. If your hips turn correctly, your trail knee should hold its position as you wind your torso and shift your weight.

Remember, keeping the trail knee in the correct position throughout the backswing is essential to proper weight transfer and maintaining resistance in your trail leg. Another drill that helps create the perfect lower body position is the Pinching Drill.

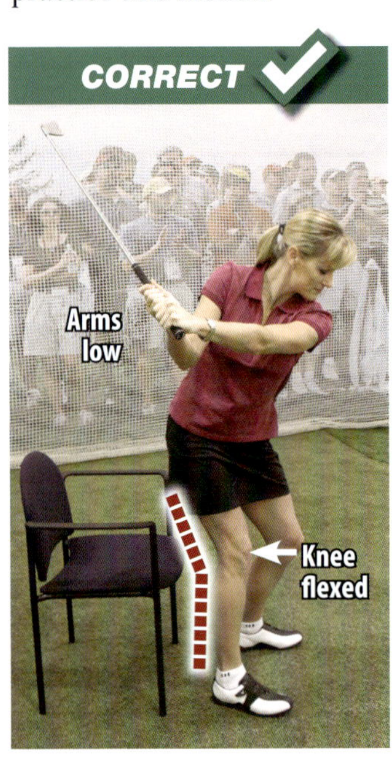

DRILL 15 THE PINCHING DRILL

While you practice the Heavy Weight Drill and learn the Pinching Drill, try to keep the lead knee pointed inward throughout the backswing. Be sure to incorporate the feeling of sitting down to generate greater power from your legs and hips. If your hips turn correctly, your trail knee should hold its position as you wind your torso and shift your weight.

One purpose of these drills is to program your mind and muscles to resist straightening the trail leg during the start of the swing. A straightened trail leg usually results from an improper coiling motion initiated from your shoulders down, instead of from the ground up. In other words, the arms cause the shoulders to tilt instead of turn, thus pulling the trail hip up. As the trail hip rises, the flex in the trail knee straightens into an undesirable "locked" position. The old axiom that "the hip bone's connected to the leg bone" certainly holds true here. It is easy to see the disastrous effects caused by starting your swing with the arms and shoulders, instead of your core. The upper body actually pulls the lower body into incorrect positions.

INCORRECT

INCORRECT

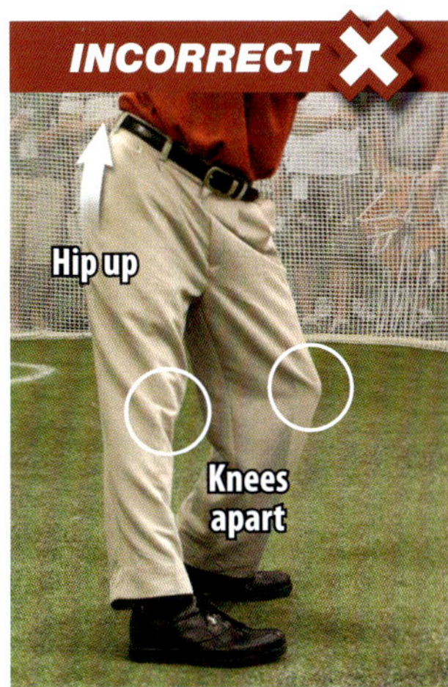

Stablize Your Knees

DRILL 15

THE PINCHING DRILL

This drill adds stability to the trail knee while promoting weight transfer off the lead knee.

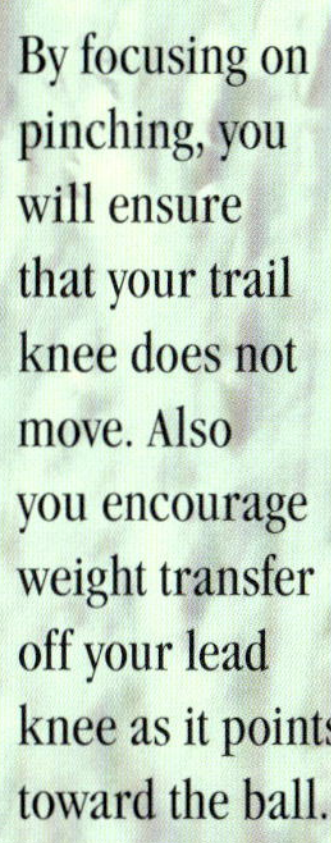

Once you have learned to sit into your trail leg, it is very important to feel the weight come off your lead knee. A subtle pinching of the knees accomplishes two great positions with one thought.

By focusing on pinching, you will ensure that your trail knee does not move. Also you encourage weight transfer off your lead knee as it points toward the ball.

To feel the pinch, place a child's ball between your thighs just above the knees. (A) To hold the ball in place you'll be forced to pinch your knees together slightly. If you have a ball smaller than this, place it higher to achieve the same feeling. Once you have the ball in place, watch yourself in a mirror (B) while practicing turning and shifting just as you did in the Heavy Weight Drill. Keep your lead hip high and make sure you transfer your weight off your lead heel, leg, and hip while "sitting" into your trail knee.

Two additional mental pictures to help you learn the correct coiling windup are the billfold pocket and the coil crease.

"Think billfold pocket," advises Don. This anecdote demonstrates a verbal cue. "I remember studying Tom Watson's swing one year at the Disney Team Championship. In this case I had to fight a crowd just to get to a place on the ropes where I could see Watson clearly. The only problem was I was behind him – not where I wanted to be to study his swing. But as I watched him swing from this unplanned perspective, I noticed how his right rear (or billfold) pocket seemed to turn in and lower slightly as he coiled on his backswing. On two previous occasions I had read golf swing research maintaining that the proper swing motion begins in the trail hip. I believe this is true and that it is a relaxing of these muscles that actually triggers the swing. When practicing the Heavy Weight and Pinching drills, try to feel this sitting position by focusing attention on your billfold pocket and repeating the verbal cue 'sit' to initiate the turn. Try relaxing the muscles of your trail hip to encourage the 'sit.'"

WATCH THE POCKET

Another point of reference that might help achieve the correct position is the 'coil crease.' "Observe the trail hip of good golfers and you'll see a crease in their pants starting in the groin area and running up to the front pocket of the trail hip. This crease is caused by the correct coiling or sitting position of the trail hip and leg, as previously described. Also notice the positions of the spring-like trail hip and leg. "If you can achieve this powerful position, you'll be amazed by how much more spring and power you possess when you change directions at the top of your backswing and move effectively through the hitting zone and into your follow-through."

LOOK FOR THE COIL CREASE

Hip Turn

DRILL 16

LEVEL HIPS DRILL

To further refine and study the movements established in the Heavy Weight and Pinching drills, try this additional exercise.

You'll need some sort of straight stick like the handle from a broom or mop. Hold the stick in front of you in your fingers, with your thumbs looped either in your front pockets or through belt loop holes on either hip.

A While standing in front of a mirror with the wooden stick aligned across your pelvic area, practice the exact motions learned in the Heavy Weight and Pinching drills. **B** Concentrate on keeping the wooden stick from tilting too much. The lead end will naturally tilt downward slightly as you turn, so don't expect the stick to remain perfectly level. It will help immensely to focus on keeping the trail hip low and the lead hip high as you turn.

"Keep repeating 'sit' as you duplicate the key points mentioned in the Heavy Weight and Pinching drills, Don advises. Once you've mastered the sitting motion, you will want to program the feelings into your brain's kinesthetic memory by oscillating back and forth between flexed and un-flexed, tight and loose, coiled and un-coiled. The feeling you want is almost like bouncing to-and-fro."

REPEAT THESE MOTIONS UNTIL YOUR MUSCLES FEEL FATIGUED.

DRILL 17 THE PUNCH BOWL DRILL

The drill will help you overcome the natural tendency to tilt the shoulders excessively toward the ground during the take-away. "As you practice this drill, you'll find it much easier to keep the punch bowl level if you feel as if your trail shoulder stays low while your lead shoulder stays high, just as in the level hips drill", says Don.

He also encourages use of a verbal cue ("punch bowl away") with this drill and suggests three sets of 30 repetitions before you move on. "Excessive dipping (❶) of the lead shoulder toward the ground causes an incorrect transfer of weight that, in turn, distorts proper spine angle."

When practiced correctly, the drill helps properly position the upper torso and weight more directly over the trail hip or leg, while releasing most of the weight and pressure from the lead leg and hip.

"I personally feel a better name for the 'one-piece take-away' would be the '*every* piece take-away,' says Don. Our desire is to use every muscle in the body, not just one muscle or one group of muscles."

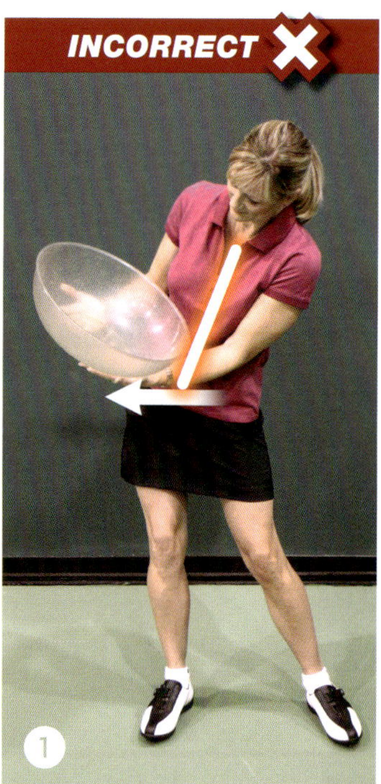

"... a better name for the 'one-piece take-away' would be the '*every* piece take-away.'"

Stable Shoulders

DRILL 17
THE PUNCH BOWL DRILL

To maximize the benefits of this drill, actually use a punch bowl or any bowl of similar size.

Ⓐ Hold the bowl level in front of you with both hands. Pinch your elbows gently in and let them touch your rib cage. Repeat the exact motion you learned in the Heavy Weight Drill (page 41).

Ⓑ During this drill, however, your concentration should be focused on keeping the punch (real or imaginary) in the bowl. To accomplish this, study your positions in a mirror and keep the top of the bowl level, starting with your arms and hands directly in front of you as you coil away from the target.

Practicing the backswing motion in this manner will help you learn what is often referred to as a one-piece take-away.

Stable Shoulders

DRILL 18
THE LEVEL SHOULDERS DRILL

Golfers take their first swings bending at the waist to hit the ball. Without proper training it is very easy to "dip" or "tilt" the shoulders on an incorrect plane in relation to the spine.

To learn how to rotate your shoulders on the proper plane, hold a broom handle or stick across the tips of your shoulders.

Ⓐ While standing straight up, make a full shoulder turn, keeping your spine perpendicular to the stick and parallel with the ground. (Look in a mirror)

Ⓑ Without changing the 90° relationship between the broom handle and the spine, tilt forward from your hips as in The Clearance Drill (page 36) and The 5-iron Drill (page 38).

Now reverse the order of movements. Start with your spine tilted forward and hips out, again make your full shoulder turn. When performed correctly, most people, even with their spine tilted forward, feel as if their shoulder plane is parallel with the ground. With your spine tilted forward, feel your trail shoulder low, and your lead shoulder high.

DRILL 18 THE LEVEL SHOULDERS DRILL ▲

During the early stages of learning a *Baseball Golf* swing, your spine angle is vertical. Your arms swing around the spine. The more you tilt your spine to face the ground, the more your arms begin swinging up and down, allowing you, as demonstrated earlier, to be the pen and the rubber band (pages 32-33). These two positions appear different only because of the tilt in spine angle.

After performing the Level Shoulders Drill correctly, take a moment and try the same turn incorrectly by lowering your lead shoulder toward the ground. In doing so, you should feel discomfort in your torso, including your ribs, back, and midsection. Notice that your hips slide away from your target to ease the pain, resulting in the improper lowering of your lead shoulder. Don encourages you to execute this turn both correctly and incorrectly focusing on the difference in the correct and incorrect motion.

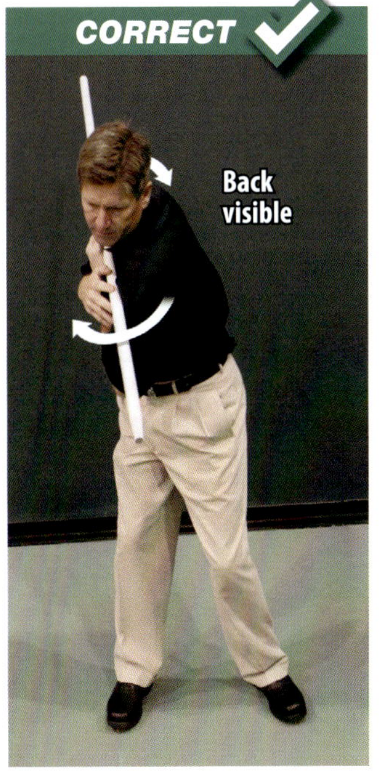

We've been giving you tools to improve your swing, but let's take a minute to discuss some commonly-accepted golf axioms that cause problems. "Most problems are born from from three clichés passed down by golf instructors through the years. They create golf swing demons that must later be exorcised."

The culprits are:

1. Keep your head down.
2. Keep your head still.
3. Hands to the sky.

Don is convinced that trying to keep your head down is an open invitation to destructive muscle tension. "It promotes a tendency to lock the chin in position too close to your chest.

Other problems, beginning with a restriction in your lead shoulder, leave it nowhere to go but down. Some students even lock their chin to their chest trying to keep the head still," says Don. "Either way, attempting to keep the head still usually leaves people with the feeling that they should not move at all – which prevents a fluid weight transfer and full turn away from the ball. Unlocking your chin and head keeps all these swing demons safely away allowing enough clearance under your chin for a proper shoulder turn."

For some time students and beginning golfers have tried to emulate pro golfers they admire who possess swings developed early in their lives when their bodies were both flexible and athletic. Most tour players have swings that are longer and more extended than what any beginner and most amateurs should attempt. Trying to reach your hands above your head on the backswing, or get the club to parallel to the ground, can induce disastrous results that keep most golfers from reaching their potential.

Don explains: "Early in my playing career, I struggled long and hard with trying to swing too upright in a hands-to-the sky fashion, only to ultimately learn that I couldn't be successful swinging my hands up this high. "Lifting the arms to achieve an upright position with the club causes the trail elbow to fly up, the trail shoulder to follow, and the lead shoulder to dip. As a teacher I've seen the same problems in my students. The average person would be better off emulating the flatter, around-the-body swing plane styles of Lee Trevino or Ben Hogan rather than the hands-to-the sky styles of a Johnny Miller."

With these factors in mind, concentrate on your lead shoulder and lead hip while again practicing the preceding exercises in this chapter. Turn your lead shoulder under your chin. Compare this top-of-the-swing position with those of some of golf's great players. You will notice that you are now similarly poised to strike the ball from a pro-like position conducive to the power and precision outstanding golfers achieve. They've learned to effectively and efficiently use the big muscles of their torsos and legs to generate the force in the swinging action of their arms, hands, and club. And now, so have you!

"As I've mentioned before, I often attend PGA Tour events to study professional swings," says Don. "People in the galleries never fail to shake their heads in astonishment and say things like, 'He looks as if he is hardly swinging.' They're amazed by how the ball just explodes off the clubface in a seemingly effortless swing. We admire these professional golfers because they make the swing look so easy. When utilizing the lessons in this chapter, and executing the swing correctly, it is!"

DRILL 19 THE WEDGE DRILL

If you've ever played baseball, you must have at one time placed your foot against the rubber and practiced throwing a pitch. Just as a pitcher is taught to "push off the rubber," the next two drills help you learn to use weight transfer to "push off" into powerful, repeatable golf swings.

The first of these drills is the Wedge Drill. "This drill comes with a warning label, because one of the pitfalls of using a wedge is the tendency to leave your weight on your lead foot," Don cautions.

"When performing this drill, make sure you transfer all the weight off your lead side, if only for a fraction of a second. But keep in mind that in your actual swing, a small fraction of your weight always remains on your lead side."

After you have learned the feeling of holding your trail knee and foot in place, be aware of the transfer throughout the rest of your turn. Then, program that feeling into your golf swing for more consistent ball striking.

SELF CHECK

The feeling you get from the Wedge Drill is closely related to the footwork used in throwing a baseball. Later we will use this footwork as we focus on "throwing the clubhead" into the back of the ball.

Coil and Brace

DRILL 19 THE WEDGE DRILL

The wedge in this drill is not a golf club, but a golf towel that is folded to raise the outside of your foot.

Place a wedge, such as a folded towel under your trail foot. This added measure ensures you are learning the proper technique when practicing alone. The towel helps your weight fall more toward the inside or instep of your trail foot. With your trail foot positioned this way, repeat the Heavy Weight and the Punch Bowl drills. "Sit" into the trail hip and keep your trail knee flexed as you practice.

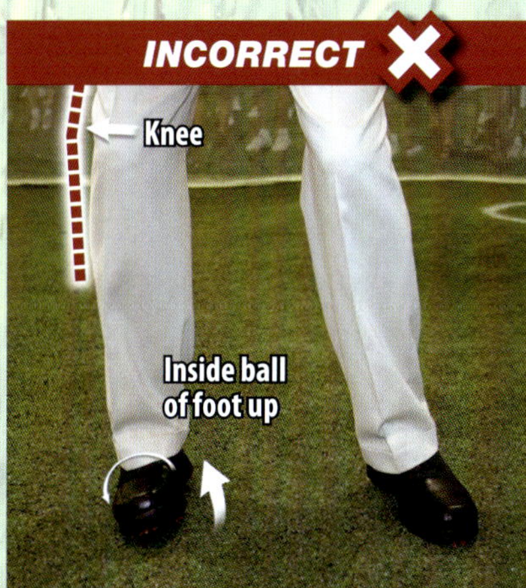

Caution: Do not use a wedge that is too thick. It's purpose is to force the pressure to the inside of your trail foot, not to lift the foot off the ground.

The Coil

DRILL 20
THE WALL DRILL

To practice a proper coil, brace your trail foot against a wall.

The wall will keep your hip and knee from swaying outside your trail foot.

Focus on making a full turn that pulls your lead knee in toward the trail knee slightly, transferring approximately 90% of your weight to the trail leg.

As soon as you feel your lead heel pull off the ground, rotate, and release into the perfect finish position, and feel how your balance is maintained within new boundaries.

For years people have been trying to keep their heads still. Instead, they should focus on the trail knee.

DRILL 20 THE WALL DRILL ▲

"In far too many students, I see the trail knee break down during the backswing," says Don. "It's easy for me to see the knee change positions as the student swings to the top of the swing. The faulty knee points away from where it pointed at the address position."

If the Wedge and the Wall drills don't correct this defect, try pointing your trail knee straight ahead, or maybe even slightly towards the ball in your address position.

A Full Turn

DRILL 21

TESTING FOR THE TRAIL SHOULDER BLOCK

Golfers get in their own way when trying to turn.

Sit on a chair with your arms crossed, pressing the stick level against the front of your shoulders while facing a wall.

A First focus on your lead shoulder. Push that shoulder around under your chin as far as you can without allowing your feet to come off the ground. Using the lead reference point of a wooden stick or driver as a sight, note the spot on the wall marked by the lead tip when you have turned as far as you can. Remember, don't lift your feet. (Keep the stick held against your shoulders and both hands pressed against their respective shoulder throughout this test.)

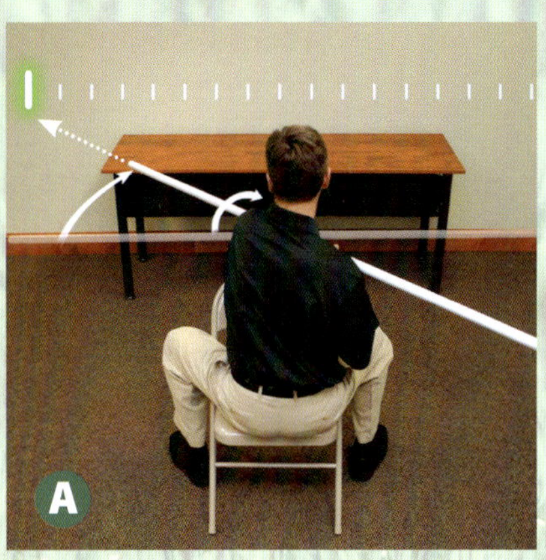

B Repeat this drill a second time, but concentrate on your trail shoulder and pull it around and behind your head as far as you can. Then, look at the wall and note where the lead tip points. More than likely you created a greater turn by pulling with the trail shoulder than pushing with the lead. If you didn't, you're one of the few.

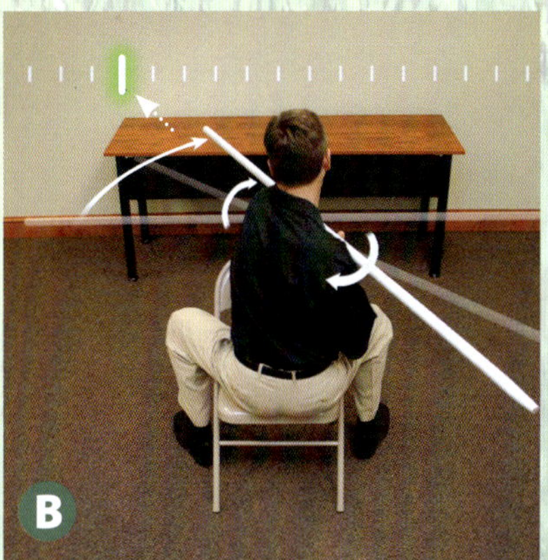

DRILL 21 TESTING FOR THE TRAIL SHOULDER BLOCK ▲

Many golfers who turn their shoulders correctly still fail to make a great backswing because they consciously or unconsciously focus on the lead shoulder to start the swing. This practice usually fails because the trail shoulder blocks the way and keeps the lead shoulder from completing a full turn behind the ball. Perform Drill 21 before reading further.

"Almost 100% of the students I asked to participate in testing this drill created more back turn when they pulled or cleared the trail shoulder out of the way for a fuller backswing," says Don. "What does all this mean to you? For a fuller (i.e. better) backswing, focus on pulling your trail shoulder out of the way. This is of absolute importance because the fuller the backswing, the greater your power." Let's move on and find out how to create torque for your new swing using The Tug of War Drill.

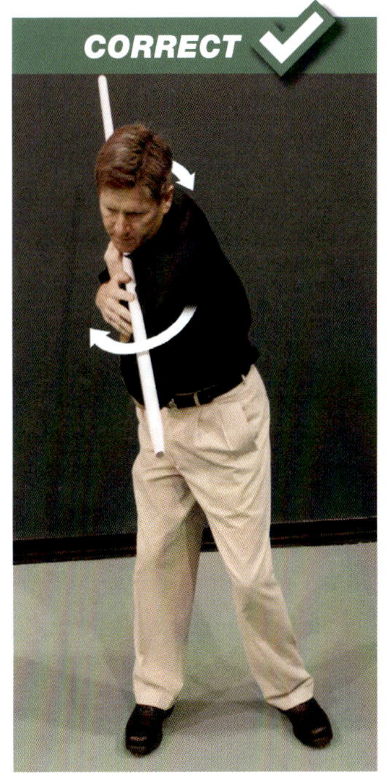

Drill 21 performed in the address position.

Reach Back

DRILL 22

THE TUG-OF-WAR DRILL

This drill will help you simulate the sensation of stretching your arms and upper torso against the resistance of your lower body.

CREATE YOUR OWN ...

Using a length of rope and with assistance from a friend, grip one end of the rope while your friend pulls gently on the other.

... TUG-OF-WAR ...

Use your feet to "grip the ground" and resist the pull against your upper torso.

Feel the sensation of being stretched back created by the tug against you.

Remember, grip the ground with your feet putting sligh

DRILL 22 THE TUG-OF-WAR DRILL 

"In a traditional tug-of-war, your opponent provides the stretch or pull on your upper torso as you concentrate on maintaining a grip on the rope and resisting with your lower body. The better your grip on the ground with your feet, the more leverage you have, and the more you can resist the pull against your upper torso," says Don. "In your golf swing you should strive to create this torque, leverage, and resistance on your own – without anyone or anything pulling against you. This is accomplished by transferring your weight onto the instep of your trail foot and using the shoulders to extend your arms.

… BY REACHING BACK TO EXTEND DURING YOUR BACKSWING.

Maintain the pressure on your trail leg and foot as you learned in the Wall Drill and the Wedge Drill.

The more you reach, the more your trail leg resists, creating more torque.

ressure on your insteps. This creates resistance when creating the "tug."

Now, that we're experienced the feeling of generating torque from our core, let's find out how to maintain proper arm position throughout the swing. Our next drill will do just that!

DRILL 23

THE SUBMERGED BALL DRILL

Designed to help you maintain a consistent radius with your arms and your body during the golf swing.

Along with the feeling of a gentle tugging from behind, you should also maintain a slight downward push with your arms. This creates a feeling of connectivity in the swing that many great teachers talk about and all great golfers possess.

To get the correct feeling:

While holding a small ball filled with air, imagine you are standing thigh-deep in water.

Pretend you are pushing downward on the ball with just enough gentle pressure to hold it submerged with your arms fully extended. You should have experienced this feeling in your arms throughout the Tug-of-War Drill.

This athletic connectivity will help you maintain proper arm positioning throughout the take-away and prevent a breakdown or improper bending of the lead arm as you turn away from the ball.

Gentle downward pressure in the arms promotes extension and a feeling of athleticism during the swing.

"With the Tug-of-War and the Submerged Ball images in mind, I want you to use your imagination and think of a different image for your arms," says Don. "I remember talking to the greatest ball striker ever, Moe Norman. He always emphasized how the body becomes like a bow and your arms are arrows."

This bow and arrow analogy is very appropriate. You've been reading about how you can train your body to use science and centrifugal force to create a repeating ball flight. Ben Hogan talked of a spring-like sequencing and compared the wind-up to the pulling of your belt buckle one notch tighter as your hips start forward to initiate the downswing. The best way to achieve this spring-like action in your swing is to practice the Tug-of-War Drill, the Submerged Ball Drill, and the Crash the Cymbals Drill (upcoming page 60) while picturing your arms stretched back on a bow string and slung forward at the target like a shot from a bow. Through learning and incorporating these concepts, my swing has become more reactionary. I aim and I fire. It's as simple as that.

"That's important. In baseball you react to the pitcher and the ball, while in golf the ball is a stationary target. You have to build this sense of reacting into your swing," says Don. Reaction is a key component of athletics. We'll learn more about incorporating this sense of reflex into your swing later. In the mean time, you can focus on an image of a bow and arrow, and as I like to tell my students, 'Stretch back – spring through.'"

SWING **NOTE!** ***Know your muscles.***

One of the great secrets to having a smooth and effortless swing is learning which muscles to use and which muscles to relax. The two groups of muscles which have the greatest impact on your swing are the motor muscles and the structural muscles. Motor muscles are the muscles easily visible when looking at your physique. The biceps, triceps, calf, and thigh muscles are motor muscles used primarily for arm, hand, and leg movements through contraction. An example of a motor muscle contraction would be a simple bicep curl. Using even a light weight, a person repeating a bicep curl would tire within just a few minutes. Structural muscles lie beneath these motor muscles and are responsible for holding our skeleton in place and erect. A person could stand or sit virtually all day without these muscles tiring. "Watch poor golfers with jerky swings, and you are watching the result of contracting motor muscles. Contrast that with the swings of today's PGA Tour stars, and you are watching the result of a swing powered from its core using the skeleton's structural muscles," says Don. Some of Don's toughest lessons have been students who spend long hours in gyms or health clubs pumping iron. Constant conditioning of the motor muscles can be detrimental when it comes to learning to swing from your core or wheelhouse. We will learn more about how the structural muscles work in conjunction with the principles of centrifugal force in Chapter 6.

The Coil

DRILL 24
THE BACKSWING FUSION DRILL

This drill is designed to help you develop a smooth backswing by focusing on three simple keywords.

You will need two balls of slightly different size, similar to those shown. A foam ball, soft rubber ball, or any such ball or item will do so long as you can hold them with a gentle pinch when placed between your extended elbows.

Begin by setting up in a golf address position – seat out, knees flexed and arms extended.

Move your body as if you are taking your backswing or turn away from the ball using the Punch Bowl Drill.

DRILL 24 *THE BACKSWING FUSION DRILL* ▲

Fusion is merely theory in the world of nuclear energy. In *Baseball Golf*, however, we are going to employ a different kind of fusion. It involves combining selected motions from the previous drills and fusing them together into a single drill – one that has the desired outcome of nuclear fusion: power.

As you perform this drill, you should feel some tension in your waist area when your lower body cannot turn any farther. Now, stretch your back by turning just a fraction farther without losing your balance or any of the coil in your lower body. (Refer to The Trail Shoulder Block Drill.) This extra stretch will create the fullest shoulder turn (or *back*turn) you can. Notice in C how you can now see the center of the back.

"You may or may not be this flexible," says Don. "But by repeating this drill you will stretch and strengthen the muscles in your hamstrings, hips lower back, shoulders, and arms to create your most powerful backswing. Continue working on this drill long after you have put this book down, and you will eventually lengthen your swing."

Your first thought will surely be that this backswing is too tight and lacks length. You'll be tempted into believing that this is not a full backswing. You may feel you are not flexible enough to complete a full turn and that you must swing back farther, even if it means breaking one of these positions.

Don't give in to temptation. Trust that this is your full coil. The picture you see of Don at right is the biggest turn he can make while performing this drill. Notice that even a golf professional like Don, who has been swinging since he was 10, just reaches his arms to shoulder height when coiling correctly. When you add a golf club to this motion, the result is remarkable. The extra weight of the golf club, combined with the momentum and centrifugal force that are naturally created during

Sit into your trail leg as in the Heavy Weight Drill; shift your weight as if you were pitching a baseball; pinch your knees; reach and stretch back.

your take-away, pulls your body a little farther, swings your arms a little farther, hinges your wrists, and helps complete your swing. Compare ❶ with ❷. This is what Don's swing looks like when performing this drill.

Now look at ❸. This overswing is the result of incorrect windup. Because this golfer didn't feel power by coiling properly, he continued to swing farther back in an effort to find power. He has lost any chance for a real coil or source of true power by trying to do too much with his arms. A goal for many golfers is to attain a long swing where the club is parallel with the ground at the top of their swing. To attain this goal they unwittingly bend their lead arm and lift the club with their arms, pulling the trail elbow away from the body. This may feel golden in your mind, but it is fool's gold. "I prefer a connected swing with width, over a disconnected swing with length," says Don. "Real power lies in more torque which, when unleashed, moves the clubhead faster and sends the ball farther."

Fusing the motions of these drills together and programming the feelings associated with this *Baseball Golf* version of fusion is very, very important. By fusing this range of connected movements into familiar sensations, we are again programming your brain's kinesthetic memory. This kind of programming allows you to eliminate unnecessary swing thoughts.

Remember, fusion is power.

Chapter 5

The Delivery

SLINGING THE HIPS FOR POWERFUL, MORE PRECISE BALL STRIKES

Previous chapters established the preliminary groundwork for a powerful, athletic golf swing. Continuing to build from the ground up, this chapter is devoted to teaching you how to swing through the golf ball efficiently and effectively like the pros. This correct turn-through motion will allow your shoulders, arms, and hands the opportunity to relax, swing freely, and deliver the clubhead to the back of the ball for distance and accuracy.

Power seems to be one of the appealing draws of golf. Just the thought of launching a golf ball with enough force to carry it two, three, or more football fields placed end to end is enough to excite most people. When students first take lessons, most of them want to increase their distance. They've watched the pros, read books and magazines, and figure there must be some sort of snap or hit at impact that makes the ball go so far. So, where is this hit, and when does it happen?

"First, the power of the 'hit' in any great swing does not occur at the moment of impact; nor does it originate in the shoulders, arms, or hands. The power is unleashed before the clubface strikes the ball," says Don. "The ball is merely positioned to take advantage of the power."

The power is released by a brisk turning of the hips and torso toward the target on the turn-through. That is what crushes the ball. The arms simply respond to this thrust of the hips and are whipped through the impact area to crush the ball. Be the pencil and the rubber band. Remember?

"Having learned in Chapter 4 how to correctly wind up and coil behind the ball, the next thing to learn is how to deliver the club back to the ball by uncoiling and releasing the torso and legs through the ball," says Don. "Notice I didn't say anything about the arms. The correct through-swing motion is best learned by training the muscles of the torso and legs first. This is what great hitters in baseball do, and this is what any golfer must do to properly strike the ball."

Training the arms, hands, and club to swing along with this motion happens later.

The correct through-swing motion is best learned by training the muscles of the torso and legs first. This is what great hitters in baseball do, and this is what any golfer must do to properly strike the ball.

SELF CHECK

In baseball, the ball is never in the same place. The batter is constantly adjusting his body's motion to make contact, sometimes getting completely off balance. Even when a hitter swings in balance, the finish is noticeably different from that of a professional golfer. The golfer finishes tall with his torso balanced directly over the lead leg. In baseball the ball is traveling toward the batter at 85 to 100 mph. Batters keep their heads and upper torsos relatively still because any movement forward would effectively increase the velocity of the oncoming ball. In golf, the ball doesn't move, allowing us the opportunity to finish our swing in a balanced, forward position every time.

Hip Motion

DRILL 25
HIP SWEEP THROUGH DRILL

Motion from our core, or the center of our mass, can be most directly attributed to the hips. This drill refines the hips' movement.

Hold the broom hooking your thumbs in your front pockets. (If you don't have pockets, tuck them into your waistband just above your hips.) Find a carpet or tile pattern on the floor to use for alignment. Anything with lines at 90° angles to each other will work fine.

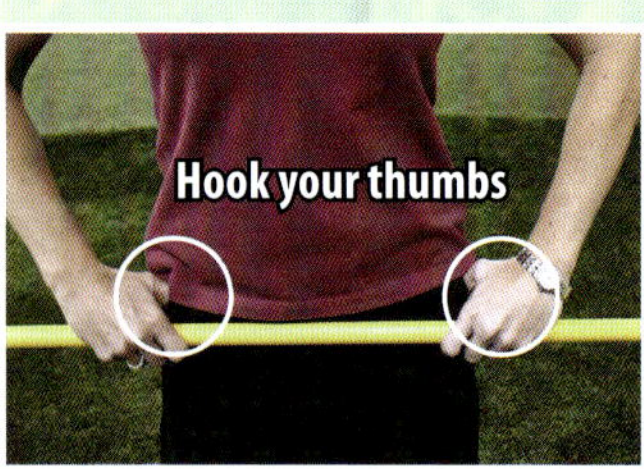

With broom in hand and thumbs secure, (A) align the broom handle with a line on the floor parallel to the target line.

(B) Repeat the turning motion from Drill 6 and turn to face the target. You have completed your turn when the broom handle has moved a full 90° from parallel to the target line, to perpendicular to the target line.

DRILL 26
THE CYMBALS DRILL

Previous drills have developed your footwork and the motion of your hips, knees, and feet. To produce long drives, we need to add some speed. The Cymbals Drill is designed to do just that!

(A) Imagine cymbals are strapped on the inside of your knees. When you turn to face the target (as in the Turn Up Drill), think of (B) crashing your cymbals together!

Use a brisk motion to crash the cymbals loudly, yet not so violently that you lose your balance. The faster you make this motion, the louder you crash the cymbals. And, the louder you crash the cymbals, the farther you will hit the ball as this rapid turning of the lower body, followed by your torso, whips the club toward impact.

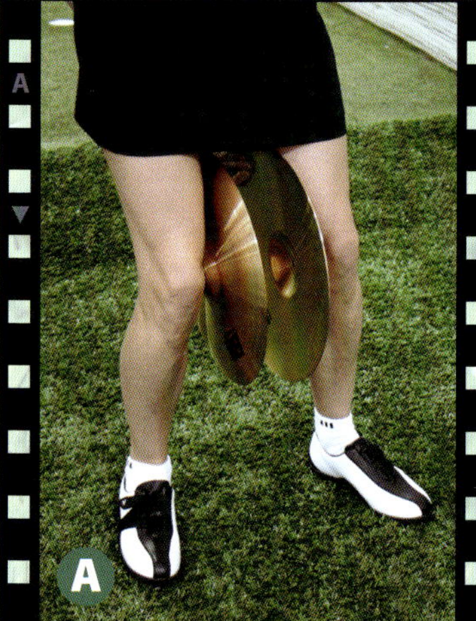

Practice the cymbals motion to the point where you are crashing them as fast as you can, as loudly as you can, finishing as tall as you can, all without losing your balance.

DRILL 27 THE TEE BALL DRILL

This is the first drill that requires you to change directions and complete your backswing, through-swing, and follow-though.

When practicing this drill, concentrate on the speed of your turn-through as we did in the Cymbals Drill. You should work to move your torso briskly through the shot without losing your control or balance. This drill will help you develop the forward swing and teach you how to correctly move through impact.

This quick turn-through motion provides the power you need to clear your hips and crush the golf ball. Practice this drill several times while standing erect; then practice from your golfing posture learned in the 5-iron Drill in Chapter 3. Turn away smoothly and in control, slowly if necessary, before turning briskly into your follow-through.

"I usually have my students repeat the Turn Up and the Punch Bowl drills a couple of times before putting the two together for this drill," says Don. "Generally this helps the

Changing Swing Direction

DRILL 27
THE TEE BALL DRILL

The Tee Ball Drill is a transitional drill that bridges the gap between simple "non-contact" motion drills and actually striking an object.

Using a tee ball and plastic bat, coil your torso away from the target **A**, then strike the ball **B** by turning briskly through the hitting area to face the target.

Turn quickly and hit the ball hard using the same movements you practiced in the Heavy Weight, Punch Bowl and Turn Up drills. As you practice, remember you want to hit the ball hard, not bunt or hit it weakly.

If you do not have access to a plastic bat and tee ball, tuck your trail elbow into your stomach and employ the same actions described above. Pretend your palm is a fly swatter and whack a fly hard enough to kill it.

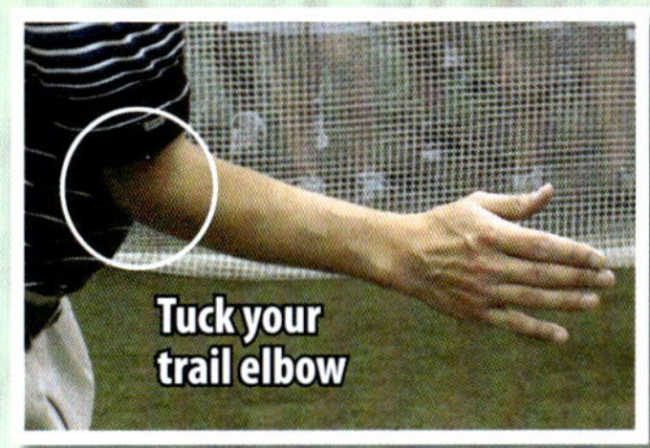

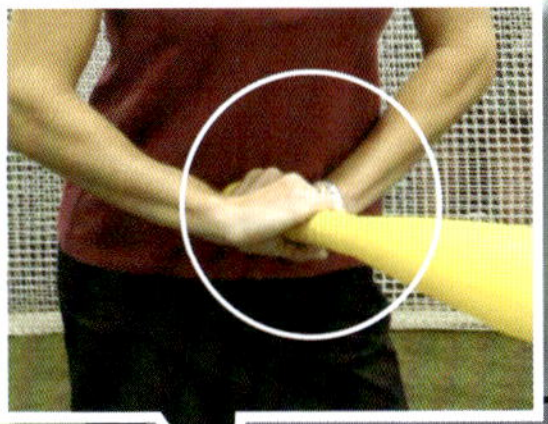

Grip the bat like this to help you use the proper muscles during the drill.

flow from backswing (punch bowl away) to through-swing (trail knee through)."

A very short backswing is best for this drill. With a short backswing, you will feel a much greater need to accelerate and create power with a brisk turn of your hips. "Concentrate on your hips when practicing this drill. The goal is to be brisk, quick, and smooth with this motion – not jerky or violent." says Don. "It has been my experience that many students turn their hips too far when coiling on the backswing."

One of the most important keys to remember is that the hips should turn only about 45° (or less) on your backswing. The rest of the coil is completed by turning your shoulders farther after the hips have become stationary. The goal is to use the larger muscles of your lower body to power the arms.

"Many golf instruction books preach restricting the hips or quieting the motion of the lower body. This is absurd. You might think tour pros' lower bodies are quiet when you observe their swings," says Don. "However, don't let the lack of visible motion fool you. Just like the carousel, the drive shaft hardly appears to be moving but that subtle motion is responsible for all that happens on the outside circle."

Start your backswing and downswing with the hips. The restriction happens only after you have begun turning your hips. You should restrict your hips from overturning beyond 45° – not from turning at all.

One of the most important keys to remember is that the hips should turn only about 45° (or less) on your backswing. The rest of the coil is completed by turning your shoulders farther after the hips have become stationary. The goal is to use the larger muscles of your lower body to power the arms.

Chapter 6

Understanding the Model Swing

WHY CENTRIFUGAL FORCE IS THE KEY TO PRECISE BALL STRIKING

Most golf instructors emphasize talking about the grip from the start. Don delays it because he is convinced it is ineffective to practice the grip until you have learned how to move the club back and forth correctly with the larger muscles of the torso. While important, the grip is the final piece to the athletic swing puzzle. We discuss the grip in the next chapter. More important than the grip itself, is understanding why and how to position the hands and wrists. Then you can use your hands and wrists in a way that allows them the freedom they need to work in harmony with correct swing principles.

"When I was 5 years old, my parents gave me an old record player. I always had more fun using it for things other than playing records," says Don. "One of the things I liked to do was spin the platter with miniature plastic soldiers on it. I soon realized that if I put the soldiers near the spindle, they'd remain in place. But, if I put them toward the outside of the platter, centrifugal force would cause them to fly off the edge. I suppose that's when I began picking up on the basics of centrifugal force and inertia. If you compare the motion of a golf swing to the motion of those toy soldiers on a spinning platter, you'll better understand the role of centrifugal force and inertia in the model golf swing."

Picture a turntable with a coin on the outside edge of its platter at the 12 o'clock position and another coin near center. If you turned the record player to the fastest setting, 78 rpm, the outside coin stays on the platter briefly, until the motor generates enough speed to throw the coin off at, let's say, 7 o'clock. If you could repeat this exercise exactly every time, the coin would fly off the platter at precisely 7 o'clock because of centrifugal force and inertia. The inside coin would remain in place.

To understand how this relates to the golf swing, imagine the coin is the clubhead; the platter is the plane of the arms as they move; the driveshaft of the record player becomes the legs and torso of the golfer. Picture a golfer at the top of his swing, coiled and ready to start the downswing. The golfer turns his driveshaft (legs and torso). The arms begin picking up speed just like the platter. The clubhead stays with the arms until the torso generates enough speed to square the clubhead and throw it off the platter (so to speak) precisely at the point of contact with the ball.

The laws of centrifugal force and inertia apply in the golf swing just as they do to the coins on the platter. This comparison makes clear an extremely significant point: Allow the clubhead to fly out of its orbit the same way the coin flies off the platter – freely and centrifugally!

"If you pattern your golf swing with this concept in mind, you'll develop a consistent pattern of release which will cause the clubhead to fly with optimum speed towards the ball in the same manner every time." says Don. "The arms are elastic (be the pen and rubber band) as the clubhead whips toward impact and strikes the ball with precision and force."

DRILL 28 THE SIDEARM THROWING DRILL ▼

With the record player analogy fresh in your mind, pretend you are a human turntable. Place a golf ball in your hand. Your torso is the drive shaft, your trail arm is the platter, and the ball is a coin. Concentrate on precision while practicing this drill. Maintain a relaxed of your trail arm. It should follow the lead of your torso as you turn through.

Practice this toss using the lower body motion and footwork developed by doing the previous drills. You should conclude every toss in the perfect lower body finish position.

Use the Force

DRILL 28

THE SIDEARM THROWING DRILL

"Catapult" your game to the next level with this swing model.

To begin, set up in your clearance position (Chapter 3) – chin up, seat out, and knees slightly flexed (5-iron Drill). Take a ball in your trail hand and hold it loosely in your fingers with the palm facing slightly to the sky. Keep your thumb from touching the ball so it is free to "fly" as if held in the bowl of a catapult.

A Position your feet on a line parallel to the target line along which you wish to throw the ball.

Reach behind you **B** with your trail arm extended as far as you can.

As in previous drills, turn your hips a quarter turn away from your target feeling your trail leg as a brace. Think "Lead heel up" or "Punch bowl away." Then briskly turn through **C** to face your target, thinking "trail heel up."

Let your trail arm swing freely in a side-arm fashion following a horizontal plane. Don't overhand throw as in a typical baseball pitch. Instead, use a side-arm motion. Keep your arm fully extended throughout the toss. Make no effort to throw the ball with your arm. Simply allow the ball to fly out of your hand when centrifugal force comes into play.

If you allow your arm to follow and give the ball "centrifugal freedom," it should fly off in the same direction time after time, as in the record player example. Try this drill with your fingers closed around the ball instead of open. This gives you a sense of control (something we all desire), but requires perfect timing of more parts. If you let go of the ball with your fingers too early, the ball will push away to the right of your target (if you're right handed). If you let go with your fingers too late, you will pull the ball to the left of your target (if right handed). We all want good rhythm and tempo, but it makes no sense to complicate precision with additional variables like muscle tension and unnecessary grip pressure.

"I prefer freedom and perfect sequence brought on by centrifugal force in my swing, and you should too," says Don. "Now let's pick up a club and learn to let the clubhead fly as freely as both the coin off the turntable and a ball from your hand."

The ball should fly off in the same direction...

... time...

... after time.

Halfway Home!

Congratulations! If you've made it to this point in the book you are well on your way to a new and improved game. Without a club in your hand we have been able to retrain the key core muscles in your body to build a foundation that will last you a lifetime!.

DRILL 29 THE FLAG POLE DRILL

You've been reading a book on building a bridge between baseball and golf, and up until now the closest thing to a bat or a golf club you've swung in earnest is a toy bat. Although it's still not time to start swinging at golf balls, it is time to pick up a club and use it for more than checking your posture.

Core Rotation

DRILL 29

THE FLAG POLE DRILL

Setting the club in motion begins directly in your core, not the arms, hands, or shoulders.

- Use a 7-iron for starters. Holding it straight up in front of you as if holding a flag, place your lead hand in the bottom position and your trail hand just above it. Don't worry about how to grip the club at this point, just take a comfortable grip. The first motion taken with club in hand is the Turn-Up Drill (page 22). Do not take a backswing.

Ⓐ Keeping the club directly in front of you, touch your elbows gently against your ribs while Ⓑ turning to face the target. Repeat this motion again, making sure it is exactly the same as in the Turn-Up Drill.

Next, Ⓐ lower the club to a point where it is extending straight out, parallel to the ground, waist high. Ⓑ Repeat the motion of the Turn Up Drill while concentrating on your trail knee. Feel as if your trail knee pushes the clubhead forward to point at the target – no more than a full 90°. Keep your elbows against your rib cage. Turn through again to face the target and "salute" it by cocking your elbows and wrists straight up. Your club should end up over your lead shoulder Ⓒ.

Concentrate on your hips, shoulders, and chest facing squarely to the target – arms bent and relaxed.

DRILL 30 FEELING THE HINGE ▼

The weight of the clubhead should hinge the wrist during the back swing. This is a very important point that will be explained at the end of this drill. This hinging action allows the clubhead to break in close to the center of the swing circle at the top of the swing. The body then begins to rotate to the target, creating a pull on the arm and the club, initiating a circular motion back toward the ball.

The Hinge

DRILL 30
FEELING THE HINGE

To feel the hinge in your trail wrist, hold your 7-iron near the bottom of the grip as if you were holding a tennis racket, a hammer, or simply shaking hands. From this position (A), hinge or cock your trail wrist (B).

Practice bending your wrist from unhinged to hinged. ▶

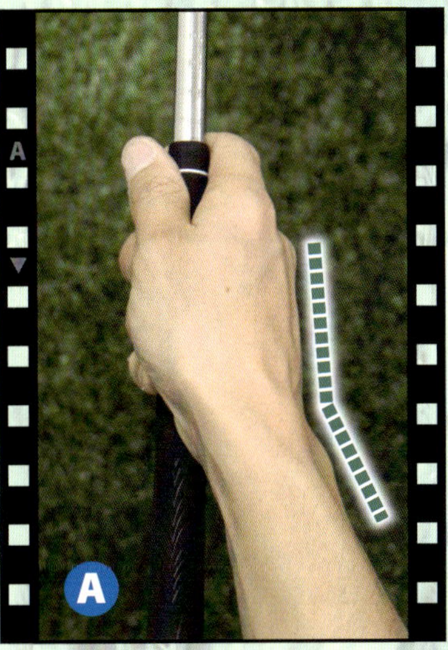

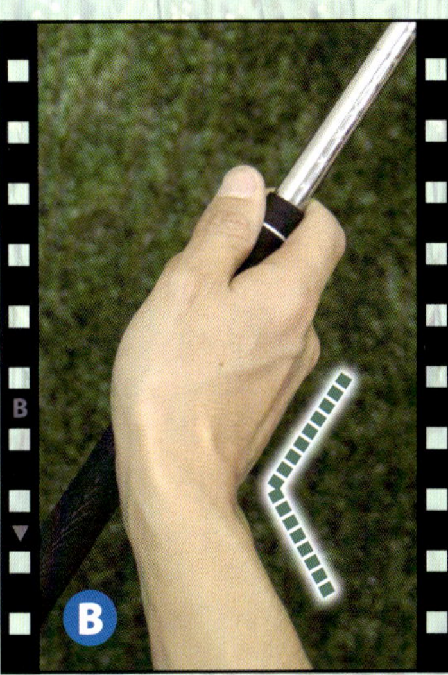

Now start in the address position with the club eight to ten inches off the ground and your trail wrist unhinged (A).

Your trail elbow should be bent and the upper arm resting atop your pectoral muscle and ribs.

Smoothly turn to the top of your swing and pause for a second to let the trail wrist relax and hinge completely.

Complete your turn-through motion without thinking about the arm or club. Concentrate only on winding into a perfect follow-through position. What happens? The body does what we have trained it to do: it rotates and uncoils to face the target. If you have made no attempt to help the club along, the trail arm and club will be put into motion by the body. The result is a perfect sequence of release: hips, torso, shoulder, arm, wrist, hand, and clubhead.

Now repeat the same motion with the lead hand only. Practice holding the club at the top of your backswing ❶. Let the club rest on your lead thumb and allow your wrist to relax as much as possible while still holding the club in this position.

Let's put it all together and perform the drill using Ⓐ–Ⓓ. With the clubhead eight to ten inches off the ground and your lead wrist unhinged, Ⓑ sweep the club up to the top of your swing while maintaining the positions used in the Backswing Fusion Drill (page 56). Once you feel the clubhead and shaft hinge fully onto your lead wrist, move briskly into your follow-through thinking "Crash the Cymbals." As your body rotates, your lead arm and club are thrown into motion by your torso. The clubhead flies out, away from the center of the circle, picking up speed on its way to the outside of the circle. Centrifugal force causes this acceleration. Ⓓ Finish tall, facing the target with your lead arm relaxed and bent over your shoulder.

Remember, as the clubhead flies out, it squares (aligns perpendicularly) to the target without using the muscles in your wrists or hands. Don advises, "Never snap your wrists to square the clubhead or to increase its speed through impact." Snapping your wrists involves too much hand movement which ruins

A relaxed lead wrist help create an ideal "hinge" at the top of your backswing with your lead thumb supporting the weight of the club.

your swing sequence. Instead, train the muscles in your arms, wrists, and hands to stay relaxed through both backswing and downswing.

If you keep the arms, wrists, and hands relaxed, the weight of the club and centrifugal force cause the wrists to hinge. As stated earlier, the wrists should hinge as a result of the weight of the club. Do not grip the club too tightly, because your wrists may not fully hinge at the top of your backswing. Achieving only a partial hinge may cause an early release at impact.

By allowing the weight of the club to hinge the wrists, you protect against gripping the club too tightly.

Relaxing your wrists eases a tight grip and tense arm muscles. This release of tension allows your arms to swing freely like the rubber band. Then, the larger muscles of your torso can be the pen, the driveshaft of the turntable, or the carousel. Get the picture? There's more, and it gets better.

Remember, it is important to feel the clubhead during the swing. If the wrists are cocked by the weight of the club, you can't help but feel the clubhead at the top of your swing. If you trust the swing that you've developed using your core, you will no longer feel a need to control the club with the smaller muscles of your forearms, hands, and fingers. The more you swing this way, the more you will develop the confidence to strike the ball with speed and precision.

"Do I push or do I pull?" is a very common query from many of Don's students. Remember playing with a wagon as a child and how much easier it was to pull it as opposed to push it? When pulling a wagon it follows you anywhere. If you walk up a path you know the wagon will follow. Since you know the wagon will follow, you gain confidence knowing that you can run up the path as fast as you want and create as much speed as you want. At the same time, pushing a wagon is a very difficult proposition. A pushed wagon could easily veer off into your mom's flowerbed! So you create a level of fear and self doubt.

In the golf swing, the dependability of a pulling action is superior to a pushing action. You have learned how larger muscles in your thighs, hips, and torso provide the pull. As your torso turns to the target, it pulls your arms, hands, and club toward the ball similar to pulling a wagon. The ball lands in the fairway not the rough.

Tipping Action:

Now that you understand how the clubhead flies out to strike the ball solidly time after time, it's also important to understand how the clubface can approach and square itself to the ball time after time.

"In a model golf swing, the clubhead is smarter than we are. Maybe that's why they call it the clubhead. It has a mind and a genius all its own. If you don't impede it, the clubhead is designed to open, square, and close by using centrifugal force as its compass. The golfer must avoid trying to guide and control the club with the hands and arms. This mistake that engages muscles only serve to slow the clubhead down," repeats Don.

The clubhead has a built-in, top-heavy load designed to roll over at precisely the right time as it speeds through the bottom of the swing arc. It's not unlike a Hollywood stunt driver filming a scene that requires a truck to tip while speeding through a sharp curve. The driver knows that if the load is top-heavy, the truck will flip over in the same place every time a specific speed is reached.

This is precisely what should happen at the bottom of our golf swing. As the clubhead flies toward the ball and "rounds the corner" the top-heavy clubhead is too much for the shaft and hosel to control. The toe of the clubhead flips over the hosel on the outside of our swing circle, naturally squaring the clubface to the ball whether you are swinging at 60 mph or 120 mph like Tiger Woods.

"I've heard every complaint imaginable from students whose swings won't work because they cannot square the clubface," says Don. "I can assure you that your clubhead, like the truck, is flipping over. The problem is that it is flipping over and squaring up at the wrong time. If you have an outside-in swing path or come into the ball on too steep an angle, the bottom of your swing arc is more than likely in front of where you have positioned the ball. Therefore, the clubface closes too late and your ball pushes or slices."

Notice in ❶ how the shoulders are in an open-to-the-target position. This position can cause an outside-in path. Many golfers have elements in their swing that produce an outside-in swing (such as open shoulders, shoulder domination, poor footwork, an arms-dominated swing – the list goes on).

"It doesn't matter what the cause. When your swing is outside-in, the bottom of your swing arc is probably forward of your ball position," says Don. "You'll always struggle to square your clubface in time with this kind of swing arc. When high handicappers swing in this manner, I can see them strain, pull, push, jump, and lunge trying to square the clubface."

> **When pros swing this way we marvel at how effortless their swings look. It is effortless because a centrifugal release does not require muscular effort to close the face of the club.**

Now study ❷ and ❸. If you are one of the majority who push, slice, or fade the ball using the outside-in swing path described in ❶, you'll need to exaggerate an inside-out swing path as illustrated in ❷ to achieve the desired swing arc illustrated in ❸. By drastically closing your shoulders and conceptually swinging to right field as you will learn in more detail later in Drill 37, the bottom of the swing arc can be changed and the clubface will flip over centrifugally in time to square to your target line. When pros swing this way we marvel at how effortless their swings look. The swing *is* effortless because a centrifugal release does not require great physical effort to close the face of the club. But non-centrifugal release does require physical effort that may square the face, but slows the clubhead.

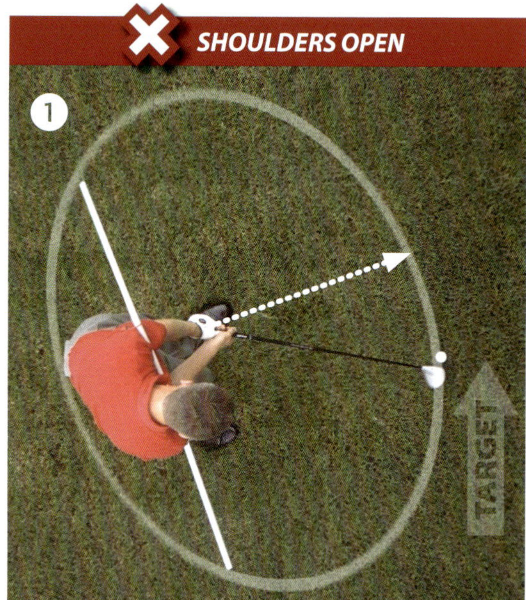

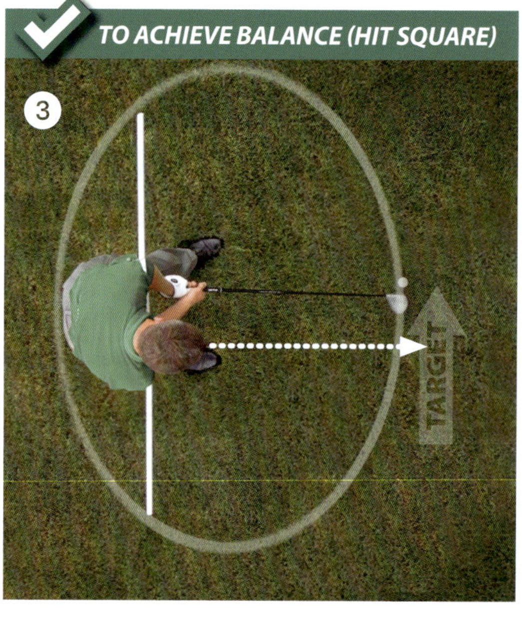

SWING **NOTE!** ***Shape your shots.***

Accomplished golfers know how to curve a ball when needed. You may intentionally slice a ball using the principles in ❶, while you may intentionally hook a ball using the principles in ❷. Later, (on page 90), you will learn nine Ball-Flight Laws. Refer to these three illustrations for clarity.

Chapter 7

Learning the Lincoln Grip

GRIP IT LIGHT TO RIP IT STRAIGHT

You have probably read about, or know the names of, the most widely used golf grips, namely the 10-Finger Grip, the Vardon Grip, the Hogan Grip, and the Interlocking Grip.

The 10-Finger Grip is appropriately named because you align your hands so that all 10 fingers touch the club without overlapping. Both the Vardon and Hogan grips vary from the 10-Finger Grip with unique finger overlaps. The Hogan Grip is formed by the little finger of the trail hand overlapping the crease in between the forefinger and middle finger of the lead hand. The Vardon Grip overlaps the trail little finger directly over the forefinger of the lead hand. The Interlocking Grip simply crosses the little finger of the trail hand under and between the forefinger of the lead hand.

"I prefer what I call the Lincoln Grip, named after our 16th president – not because he invented it (I don't believe Abe golfed) – but because of what he's best remembered for – freedom," says Don. "The most important ingredient a grip must possess is a lightness of touch that provides freedom for the clubhead to swing. You've learned the club has the ability to swing itself correctly through the golf ball if you let it. By allowing the clubhead freedom, you'll achieve a more consistent swing. That's right. I said if you want control of your golf ball and the direction it is headed, then you have to surrender control."

10-FINGER GRIP

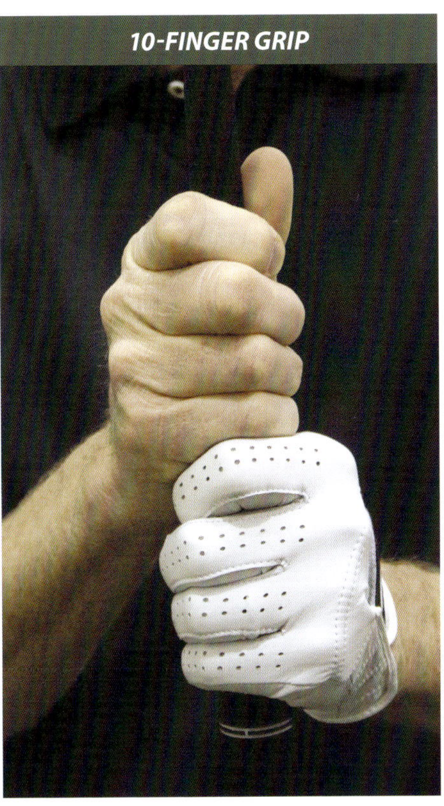

INTERLOCKING GRIP

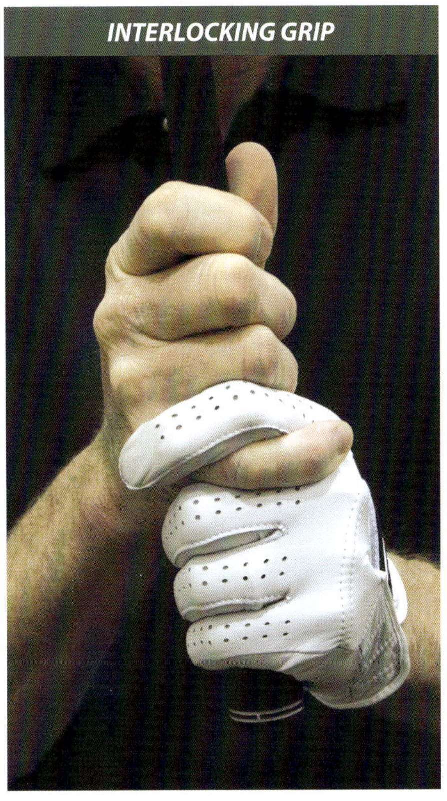

VARDON GRIP

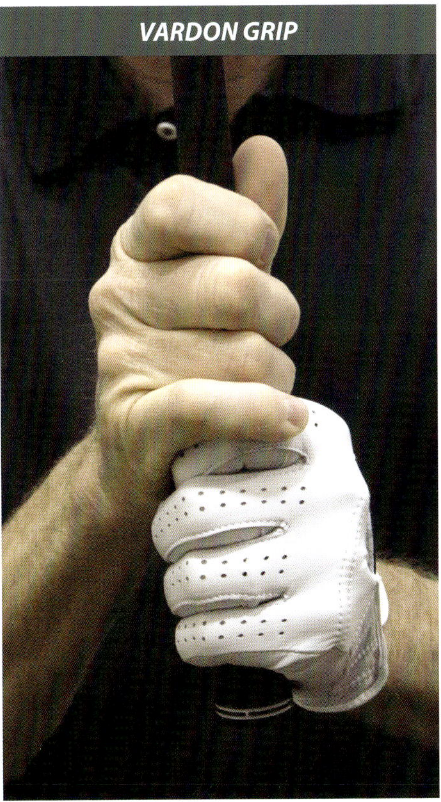

HOGAN GRIP

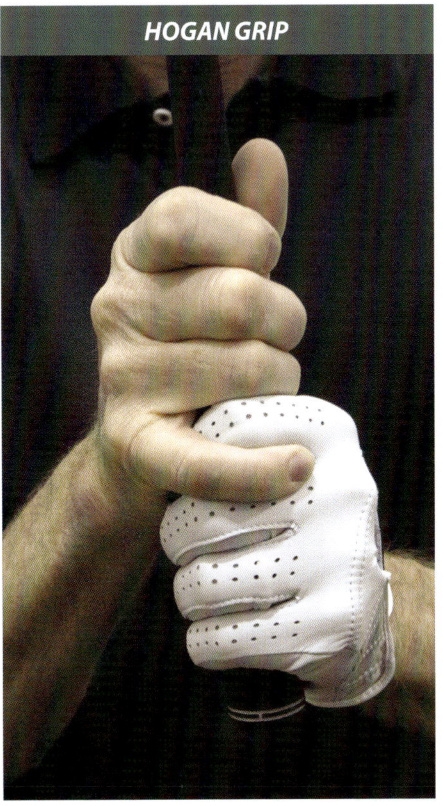

"The biggest secret, to controlling your golf swing by not trying to control it, is not to grip the club too firmly in an attempt to control the face of the clubhead," says Don. "Just allow the clubface to do what it wants – what it's designed to do – as you turn back and through. If you grip the club correctly and don't get the desired result, then you need to alter some other facet of your motion, posture, or alignment. Do not attempt to manipulate the clubhead with your hands."

Prior to gripping the club, it's important to understand proper clubhead alignment. To align the face of your club properly, use the bottom, leading edge of the clubhead. Align the face perpendicular to the intended target line. Do not align the top edge of the clubface. This is a common mistake among beginners and some high handicappers that will result in the face of the club aligning to the left of your target (for a right-handed golfer), de-lofting the club.

THE BASIC GRIP: To determine how you should align your fingers and hands on the club, Ⓐ first locate the center of your lead wrist hinge. Do this by holding your lead hand out in front of you Ⓑ, cock your lead wrist upward, and point your lead thumb straight up as you would to hitch a ride. Using your trail forefinger, trace a line down the back of your thumb to the hollow area or low spot (called the *hinging point*) adjacent to the large tendon at the base of the thumb, near the wrist.

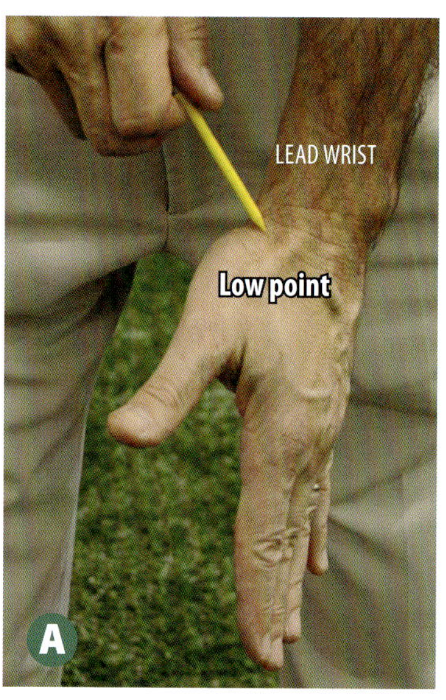

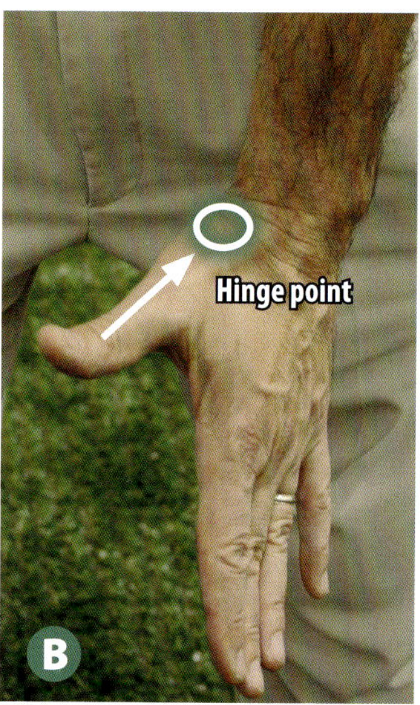

When you place your lead hand on the grip, make sure the hinging point is directly over the top of the club shaft ❸. When positioned directly over the top of the club shaft, the hinging point will accomplish three very important things. It will:

- Support the club at the top of your swing.
- Help create maximum leverage on your downswing.
- Balance the joints and muscles.

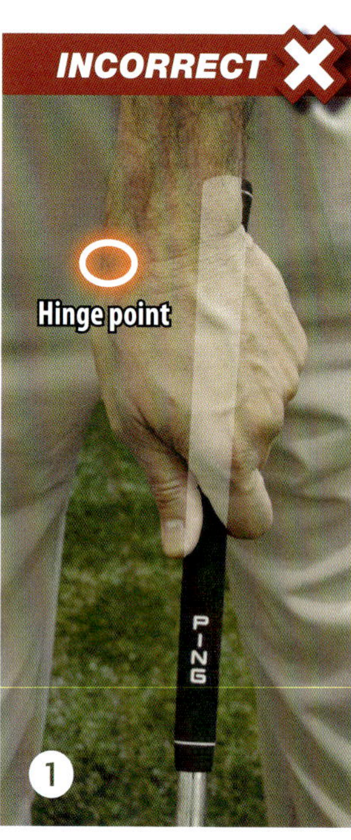

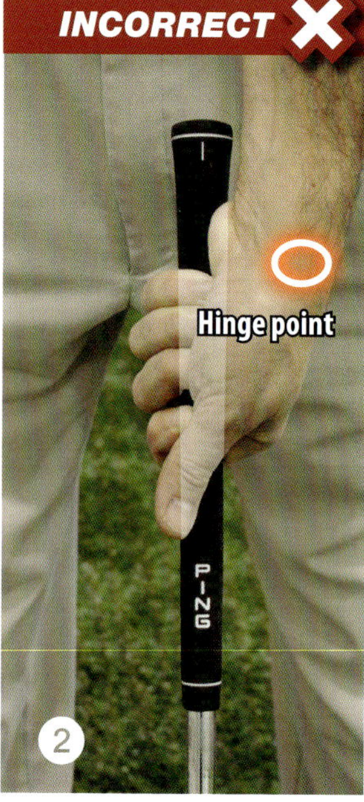

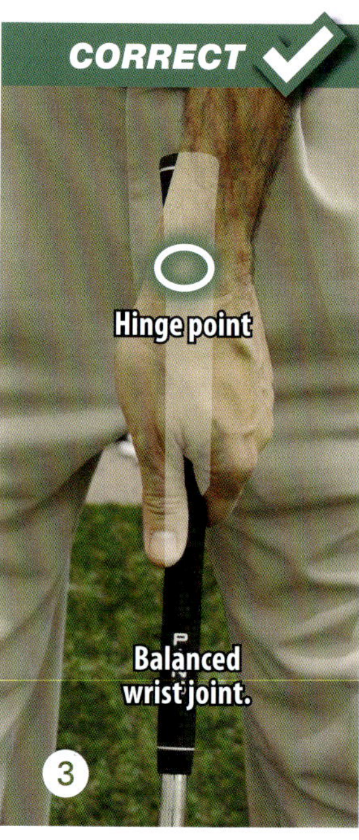

INCORRECT

Gripping the club too tightly restricts proper hinging.

If your lead wrist or hand is improperly placed on the golf club, you may have an undesirable position at the top of your swing. Often, a cupped position results when the lead hand grips the club in the stronger, closed position (❶ and ❹). Also, a hooded or shut position may occur at the top of the swing when the lead hand is placed in the weaker or open position (❷ and ❺). "If you are going to err in one direction or the other, make it this one," advises Don. "I can show you several players on tour who swing from this position and play great golf." The worst possible combination would be to combine a weak lead seen in ❷ with an open or cupped position found in ❹. The most desired position ❻ results when the hinge point is aligned directly over the grip and shaft ❸.

CORRECT

HIGHLY UNDESIREABLE

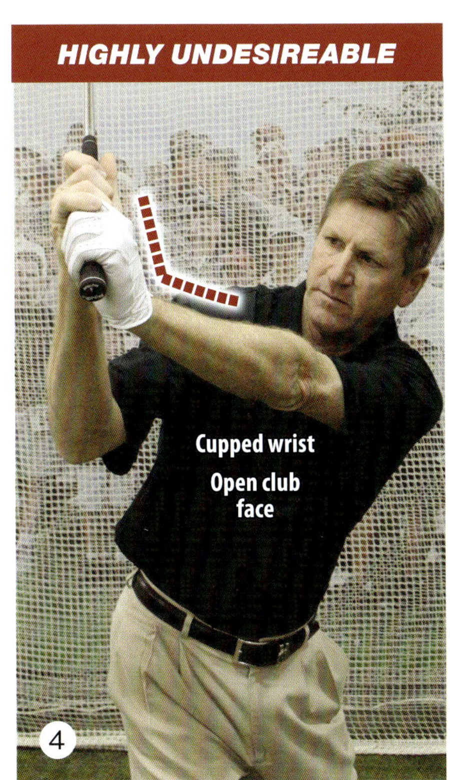

SOMETIMES DESIREABLE

MOST DESIREABLE

SELF CHECK

You should be able to hold the club off the ground by using only your lead forefinger **A**. You can feel the hinge point in action **B** by simply cocking your lead wrist straight up. It should feel as if you are lifting up on the clubhead. As you lift up, you will become aware of pressure placed under your lead heel pad.

Make sure your lead forefinger hooks around the grip. The butt end of the grip should run diagonally from the forefinger, across the palm, and under the muscle pad. A good way to assure that your lead hand is in the correct position is to check in a mirror that your lead heel pad is positioned on top of the butt end of the golf grip. Then simply close your remaining fingers together.

You may think we're spending too much time just learning how to place the lead hand on the grip. After all, how hard can it be? While it should not be difficult, it can be a problem. Don recalls a recent PGA Teaching and Coaching Summit where five out of six top instructors cited placement of the lead hand on the club as the number one problem they see among students.

This final view may help you to place your lead hand on the club correctly. Many students reach under too far ❶ to gain "control" of the club. By properly positioning the ulna bone over the shaft ❷ you can see how the center of the wrist aligns directly over the grip's center.

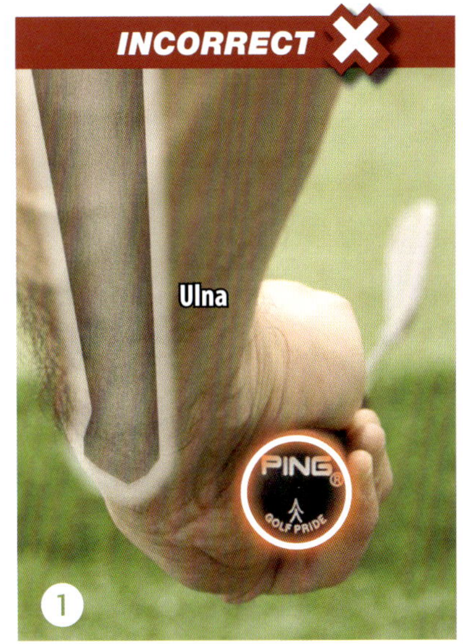

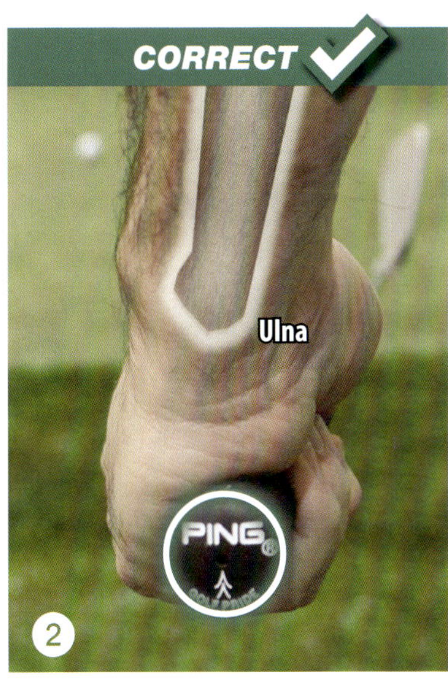

If you're wearing out gloves with holes like this, you need to take the Tee Test.

The Tee Test:

Now that you are sure you have your lead heel pad in the correct position, close the back three fingers of your lead hand around the butt of the grip. These three fingers now become the most important link to holding the club correctly throughout your swing. The tee test is a way to make sure you are correctly closing these three fingers around the shaft and keeping the lead heal pad in place throughout your swing.

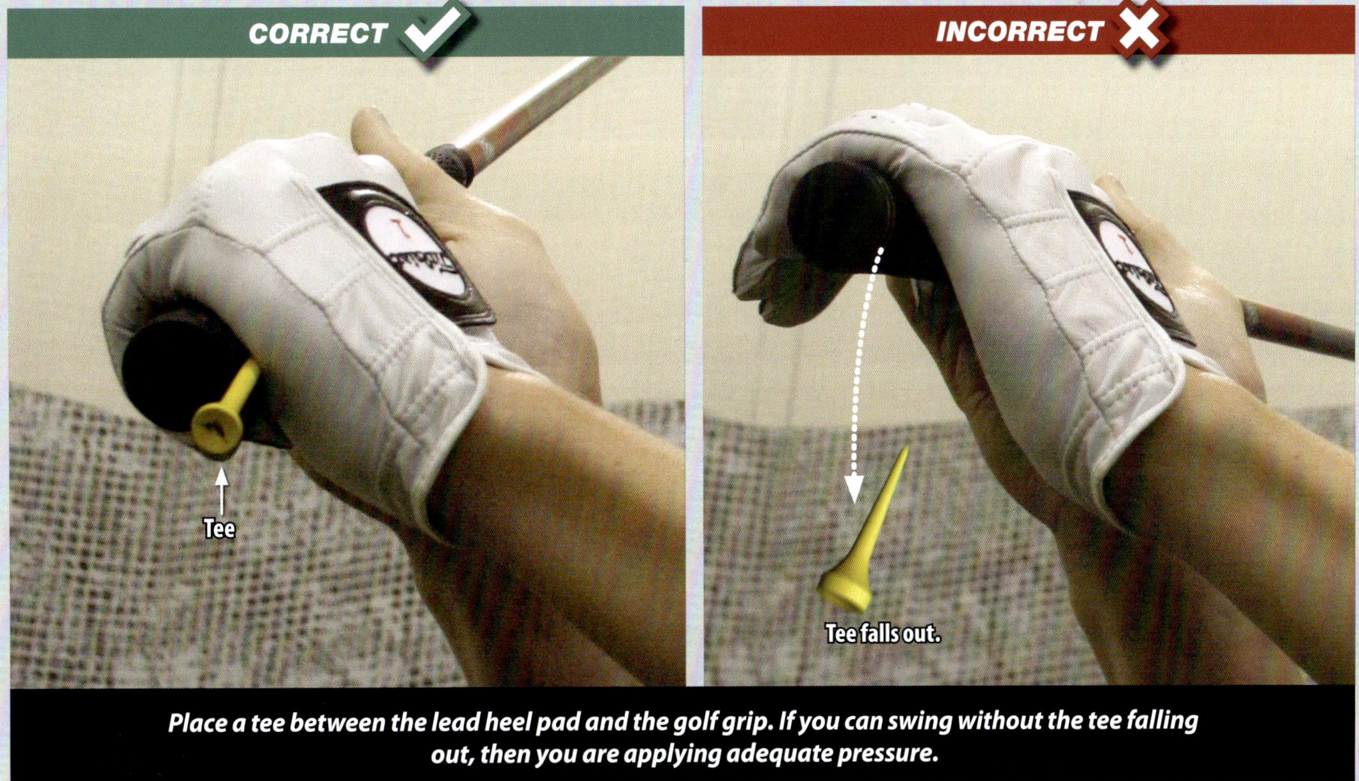

Place a tee between the lead heel pad and the golf grip. If you can swing without the tee falling out, then you are applying adequate pressure.

COMMON GRIP FLAW ▲ When placing your trail hand on the grip, do not hook the trail thumb. Hooking your trail thumb creates too much muscle tension and grip pressure. The thumb should be relaxed and straight ▼.

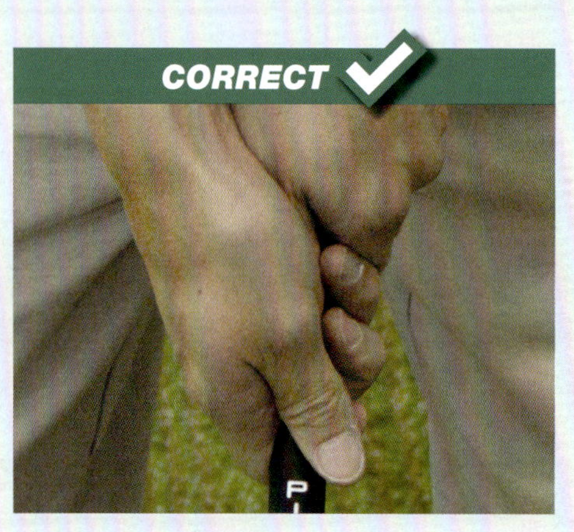

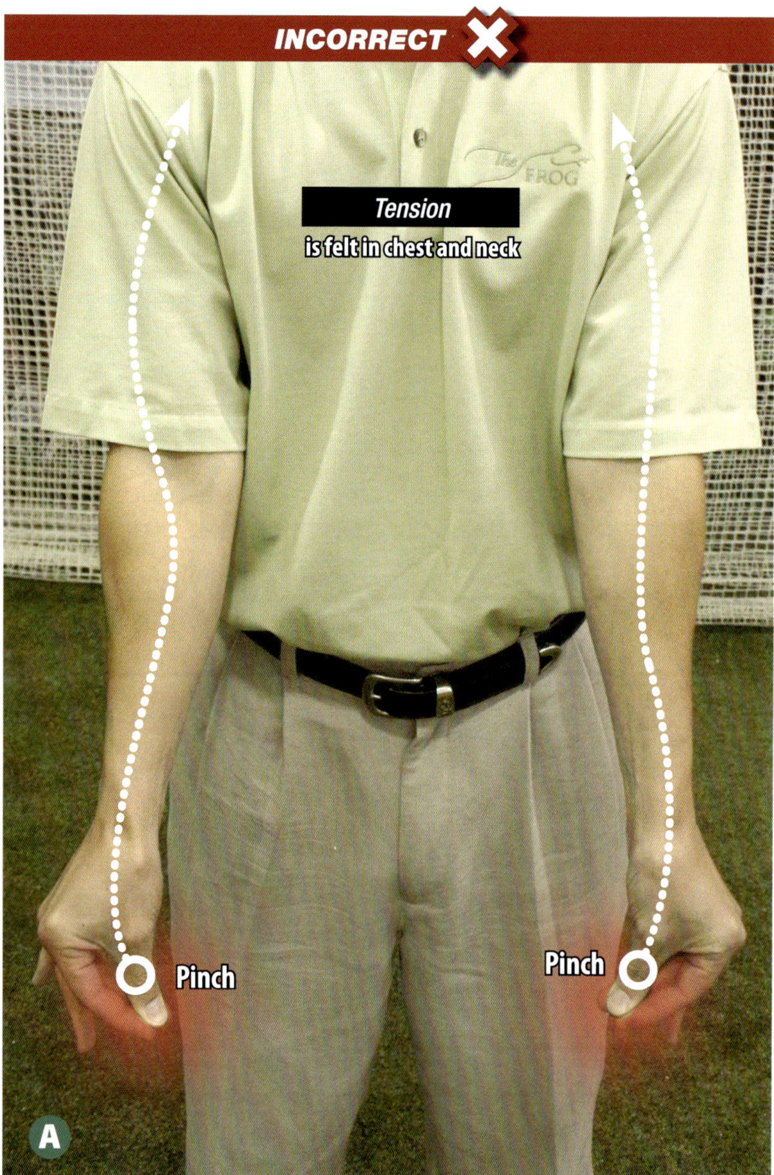

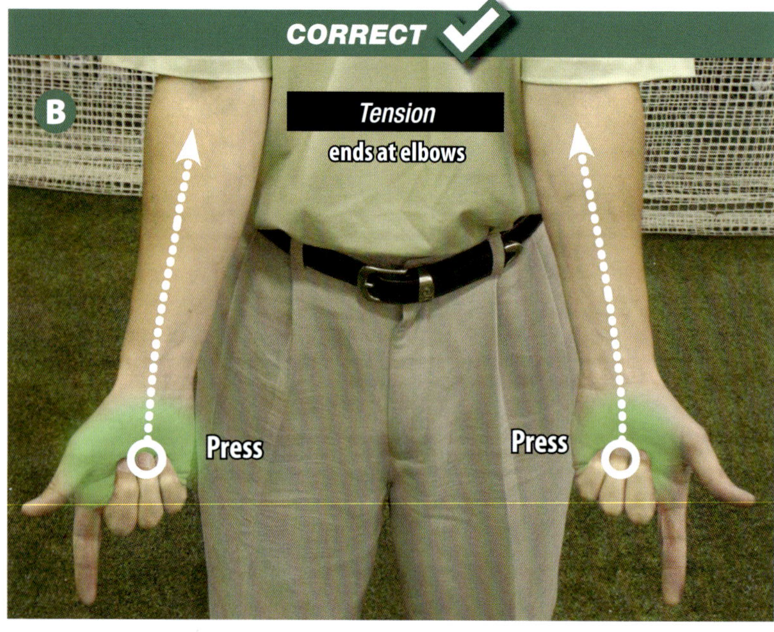

THE GRIP PRESSURE TEST ▶

To ensure that you are gripping the club with the correct pressure and the appropriate muscles, take the Grip Pressure Test.

A Pinch the thumb and forefinger of both hands together and squeeze as hard as you can. Feel the tightness run all the way up your arms into your chest and neck. This is because the long muscles, used to pinch, connect up around your collar bone. Now, relax your thumbs and forefingers, and, instead, squeeze only the back three fingers on each hand **B**. The tension in your chest and neck diminishes because these muscles attach at your elbow. This new awareness should make it easier to grip your thumbs and forefingers. Instead learn to hold the club by closing the back three fingers of your hands softly around the grip.

Place your trail hand on the grip by raising the club in your lead hand in front of you. Hook the two middle fingers of your trail hand around the grip Ⓐ. Be sure the palm of the trail hand does not touch the grip handle. Cover the trail thumb completely Ⓑ with the trail palm.

Now close your fingers around the grip Ⓒ with the little finger of the trail hand on top of the lead forefinger. The "lifeline" in the palm of your trail hand should lie on top of your lead thumb. The thumb of your trail hand should rest against the lead side of the grip. If you feel you have a good hold of the club, then chances are you're gripping too tightly or using an incorrect grip. Remember, most people grip the club too much in their palms, rather than slightly toward the fingers.

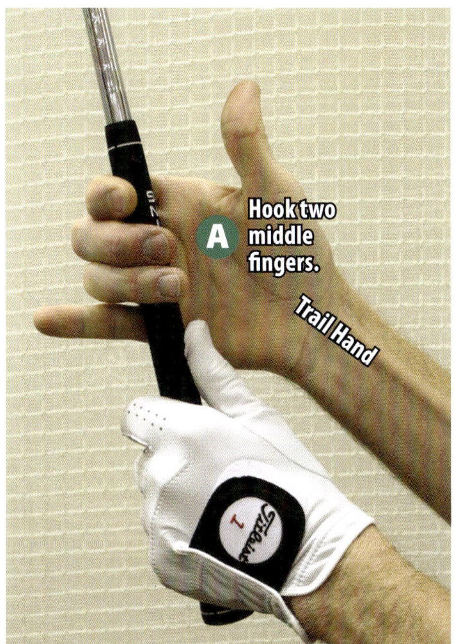

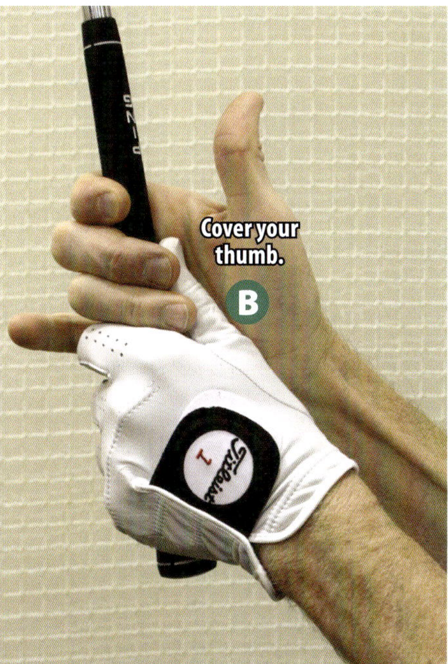

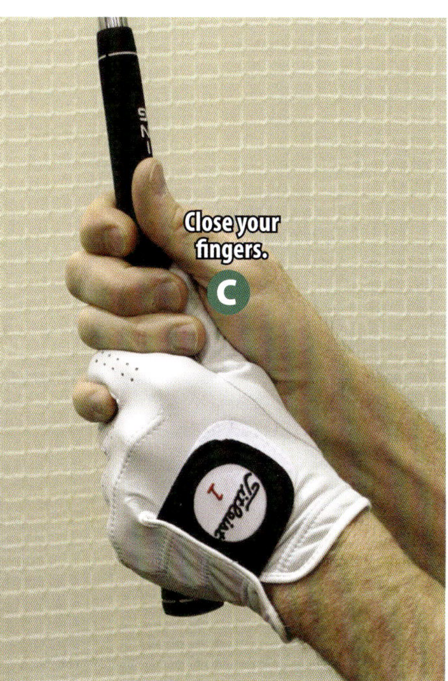

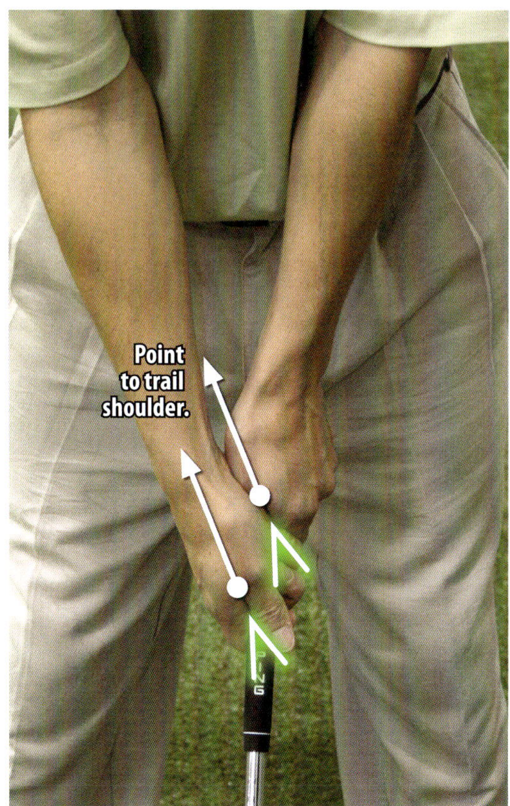

When players close fingers around the club, it's difficult to know if their hands are truly aligned in the manner consistent with good golf principles and the model swing. To check grip alignment, study the following pictures of correct and incorrect alignment patterns. To accurately assess the position of the palms, grip naturally, then open the fingers without moving either palm.

INCORRECT

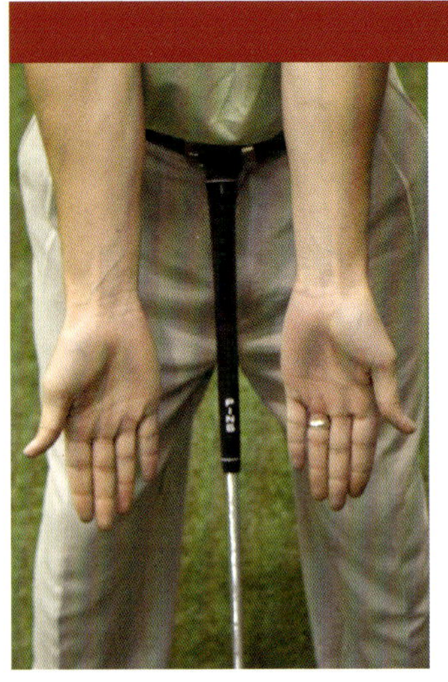

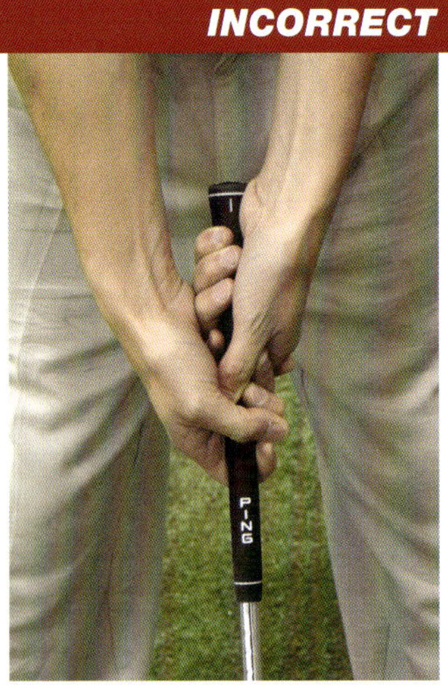

◀ ***OPPOSING PALMS UP*** generally causes this position at the top of the swing. The corresponding ball flight is usually a hook. Its trajectory is very low, sometimes not even getting off the ground.

INCORRECT

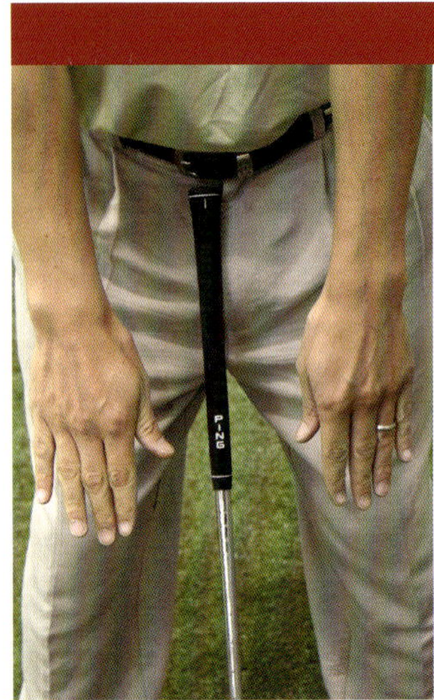

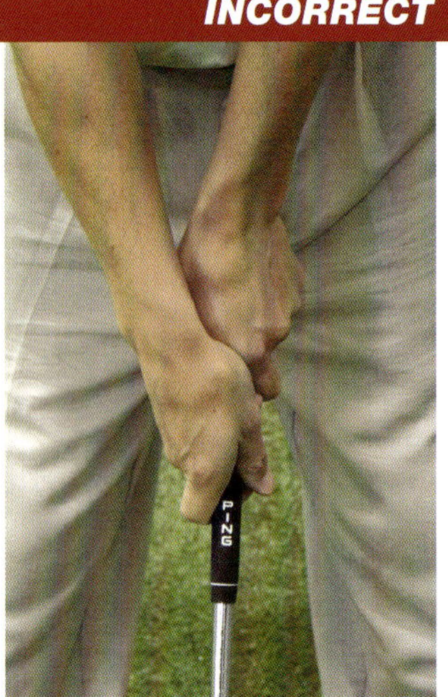

◀ ***OPPOSING PALMS DOWN*** generally causes this position at the top of the backswing. Its corresponding ball flight is usually a slice, a push or a shank (worst).

SWING **NOTE!** *Grip lightly and hinge.*

"Remember to think of your wrists as hinges. In the golf swing, that's all they should ever be. If your hands strain to hold the grip too tightly, your hinges are in effect rusted and not swinging freely, costing you valuable clubhead speed and efficiency," says Don. "And there is always the popular image of holding the grip as if it were a bird you found outside, stunned but still alive. You need to hold the bird tightly enough so that it will not flap its wings and injure itself, yet loosely enough not to hurt it. It's the same as holding an open tube of toothpaste – squeeze it too hard and you have paste all over the place!"

Applying the correct amount of pressure to the grip should secure your fingers around the grip and still allow your hinges to swing freely.

CORRECT

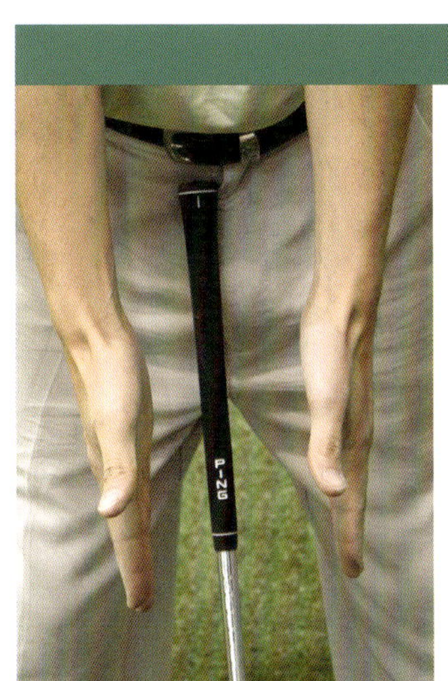

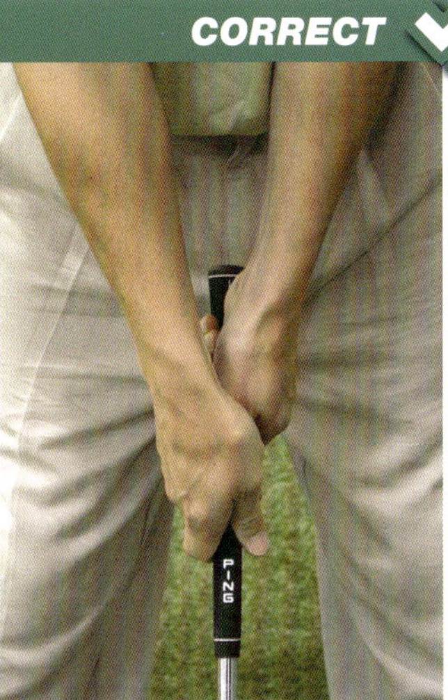

PARALLEL PALMS NEUTRAL generally produces this palm position. Its corresponding ball flight may tend to fade.

CORRECT

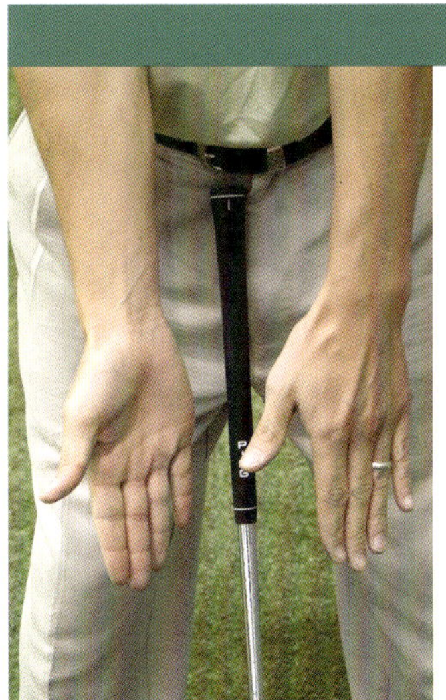

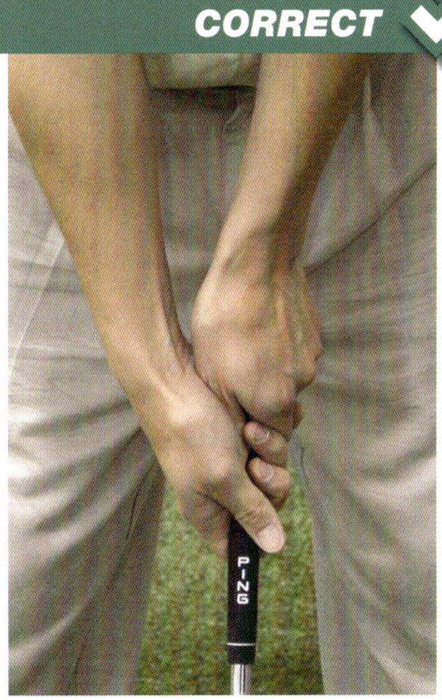

PARALLEL PALMS STRONG generally creates this palm position at the top of the backswing. Its corresponding ball flight may tend to draw.

* If right-handed

Chapter 8

Don't Blame Baseball

TECHNIQUES TO KEEP YOUR SWING ON-PLANE AND INSIDE-OUT

There's a temptation to call this chapter "Embrace Baseball," because of the various baseball swing elements you can tap into to make the process of swinging a golf club feel more athletic. Many people think the baseball swing and golf swing are polar opposites. They see the baseball swing as horizontal and the golf swing as vertical. As a result, when they begin to play golf, they develop a steep, up-and-down swing in an attempt to be un-baseball-like. Their athletic prowess is lost. They are left with a very disconnected swing that fails to coordinate the body's muscles for precision and power.

Many people blame baseball for their poor golf swings, when instead they should be embracing these skills and adapting them for golf.

"They blame baseball for their poor golf swings, when instead they should be embracing their baseball skills and adapting them for golf. That is what the *Baseball Golf* approach can do for you," says Don.

At this stage of the process, your swing development can best be accomplished while standing erect and swinging on a horizontal plane parallel with the ground – much like you might swing a baseball bat at a high pitch. From there we will gradually adjust spine angle and swing plane forward and downward toward a golf ball positioned on the ground.

The pre-set positions in Drills 31-33 and 35-37 are designed to initiate this process. They will help you coordinate proper arm, wrist, hand, and club motion by using the verbal and mental cues for movements learned in the first six chapters.

The Wrist

DRILL 31

90° OF PRONATION

To learn to swing properly you will need to understand pronation and supination.

Pronation and supination are often misunderstood words popularized in golf by the great Ben Hogan. He said they were the major reasons for his success on the PGA Tour and the "secret" to his golf swing. "*Baseball Golf* is the 'secret' to understanding them," says Don. "These terms are much more easily learned and understood by taking horizontal swings, so let's get started," says Don.

A Grip the club in your lead hand only, pointing the club straight up. Choke up near the middle of your club if it feels too heavy.

B Rotate your lead forearm without changing the position of your upper lead arm, until the club turns 90° and points away from your intended target.

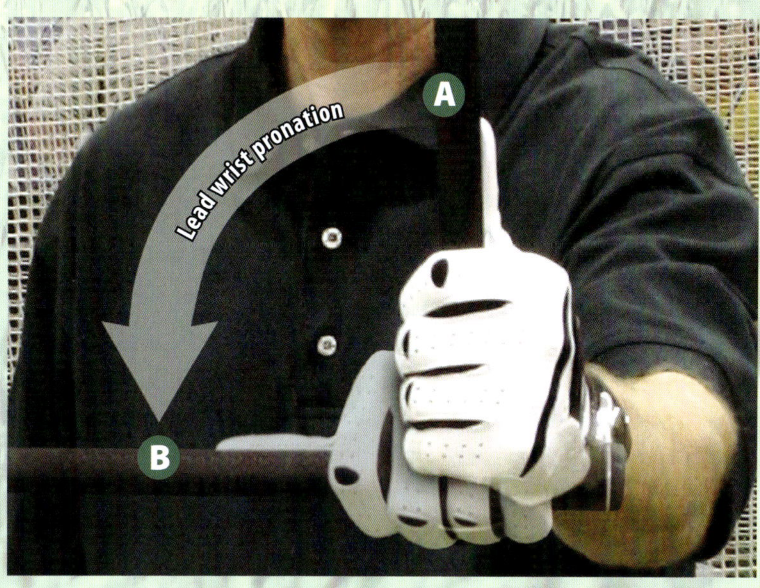

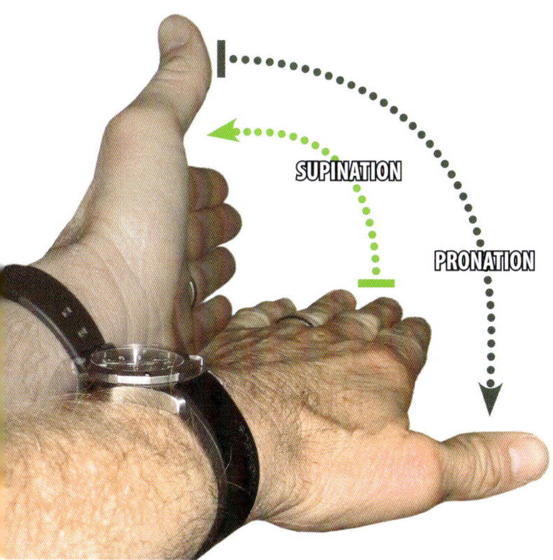

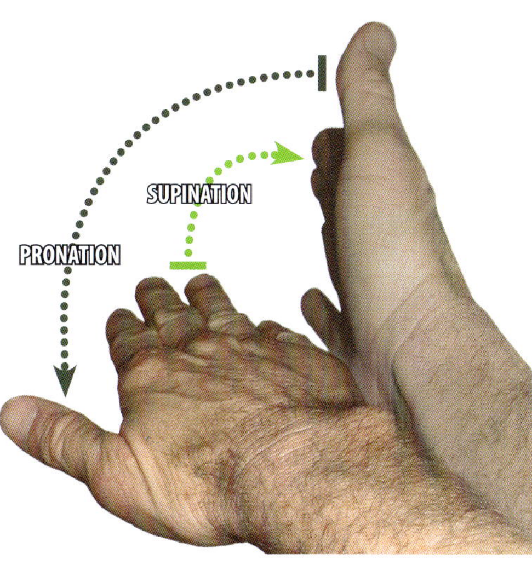

Be sure to understand pronation and supination before you begin the next drills.

Using pronation and supination will help your swing flow freely and feel more natural as you work through the final chapters of *Baseball Golf* and begin practicing and playing.

Preset Arms, Wrists & Club

DRILL 32

90° PRONATION plus PUNCH BOWL DRILL

Now add your trail hand to the club in a normal, proper grip A – but still in the vertical position described in the previous drill. B Roll the lead arm 90°. (You are still pronating your lead wrist, but for practical purposes you are supinating your trail wrist.)

C Then rotate your hips as if you were practicing The Punch Bowl Drill, using "Punch Bowl Away" as your verbal cue. Your lead arm should wind up against your chest. You have just completed your backswing. This horizontal backswing only works properly for a ball positioned chest high – just like a chest-high fastball in baseball.

DRILL 32 90° PRONATION plus PUNCH BOWL DRILL ▲

Most people refer to this horizontal swing negatively as a baseball swing. But remember, all these drills are designed to help you realize and also feel that the only difference between a baseball swing and a golf swing is the spine angle – upright for baseball, tilted for golf. Once you understand and begin to feel the similarities in your baseball and golf swings, you can tap into the comfort of your horizontal baseball swing and incorporate it into a greater sense of athleticism as you alter your spine angle for golf.

The Wrist: Follow-through

DRILL 33

90° SUPINATION *plus* CRASH THE CYMBALS DRILL

Now it's time to practice the follow-through. However, this time roll (supinate) your lead forearm 90° toward the target.

A Begin in the same start position as Drill 32. Using the Turn Up Drill motions, (think "trail knee up" as your verbal cue), turn through **B** to your follow-through position. Concentrate on bringing the trail hip forward, as in Drill 35 (page 60). The clubhead should follow a smooth, horizontal plane **C** winding up behind your body.

Next put Drills 32 and 33 together. Start with the backswing and repeatedly swing the club back and around your body. Don't dwell on the motions of your arms, hands, and club. Concentrate on coiling the torso and the follow-through. Start with the club raised in front of you and turn away – "Punch bowl away," and turn through – "Crash your cymbals." You're now using correct muscular sequence and feeling centrifugal force.

Done correctly, combining Drills 32 and 33 feels like swinging at a high fastball.

DRILL 33 90° SUPINATION *plus* CRASH THE CYMBALS DRILL ▲

Practice keeping your lead wrist flat during these drills. Continue baseball level swings, slowly tilting your spine to the ground and lowering your hands, continuing your mental and verbal cues.

You will find it is easier to train the muscles of your hips and shoulders while standing erect because your shoulders and hips turn more easily on parallel planes. Your swing will feel increasingly less natural and less instinctive as you gradually adjust your spine angle to address a ball on the ground. With your feet firmly planted on a level surface, your hips generally should rotate on a fairly level plane, parallel with the level surface of the ground. Your shoulders, which rotate at 90° to your spine, will gradually tilt more and more to the ground as you alter the angle of your spine to address the ball. The lower the ball, the greater the difference between the shoulder plane and the hip plane. This is why the rotary motion of the hips and the shoulders are best learned from the relatively erect position of the baseball swing.

Proper club position at top of the backswing is one of the most difficult things to learn and also one of the most difficult to teach. Let's take some time to help you achieve a proper top-of-the-swing position by following the sequence below.

Start with your club preset as you did at the end of the 90° Pronation plus Punch Bowl Drill (page 82).

Lower your arms until the trail elbow rests on your rib cage.

Tilt forward slightly by bending only at your hips as in The Clearance Drill (page 36).

Repeat The Backswing Fusion Drill (page 56).

You should arrive at the top of your backswing in a position similar to ❸ below.

Now take a good look at ❶. This is the position most golfers strive for – not too different from Tiger Woods or Ernie Els. The trouble is, most of us are not flexible enough or strong enough to get into this position.

Next look at ❷. This swing position occurs when golfers try to swing back farther than they are capable. Often they lift with their trail shoulder, arm, and hand in an effort to swing the club all the way up to parallel (with the ground). This extra effort and overswing throw the club off-plane and totally out of position for a proper return to impact. Notice the trail elbow flying up and the cupping in the lead hand. The roots of *Baseball Golf* sprang out of this consistent problem. To eliminate this catastrophic position at the top of your swing and begin your swing in the more powerful and "on-plane" position in ❸, you may need to exaggerate as Don has done in ❹.

This may not be what you want your swing to look like, but if you want to benefit from what you learned so far in this book, you may want your swing to feel like ❹ in order to achieve a good position as shown in ❸ and ❶.

SELF CHECK

For this, you'll need a little help from a friend. Swing to the top of your backswing allowing your lead wrist to cup. Pause and have your friend hold the club shaft firmly with both hands (A). Begin your downswing (B) by turning your hips toward the target gently. We don't want to hurt your friend. Your downswing will feel powerless and the club will feel like it is on top of your forearms.

Now try the same move with your lead wrist flat (C). As you turn your hips toward the target (D) you will feel much more leverage and power, and the club should feel like it is below your forearms (or in line with your trail forearm).

"Initiating the swing with your hands or arms can have disastrous results," says Don. "Moving the clubhead away from the ball with the small muscles of your wrists and hands will result in an inconsistent swing and/or clubhead path. If your swing follows a different path every time, control of your shots, and ultimately your ability to improve your game, will suffer tremendously."

Start your swing by using your torso. If your posture and clearance remain intact, your arms, hands and the clubhead will trace the same path from the ball, time and time again (as explained at the beginning of Chapter 2). As ❶ shows, neither the shoulders nor the lead knee have moved. But in ❷, both the lead knee and shoulders have moved. The take-away pattern is more precise. Remember, an "every-piece take-away," not a "one-piece take-away!"

As you swing the club around the body, your grip should be light so the weight of the clubhead both pronates the lead arm open and also causes the hinging of the lead wrist. This action will feel sloppy at first. The club will flop or dip onto the lead thumb when it rests at the top of the swing.

"If you want to consider the so-called cosmic elements of golf, this is where you let go of your fears and inhibitions to find your inner swing," says Don. "If you want to understand the essence of the athletic golf swing, this is where your fingers maintain a relaxed grip that allows you to get a feel for the clubhead. You can't feel the clubhead if you grip the club too tightly and flex the longer muscles of your arms."

With muscles relaxed, the weight of the clubhead pulls your swing back a little farther, hinging your wrists to their fullest extent. This is a good thing! Swinging in this

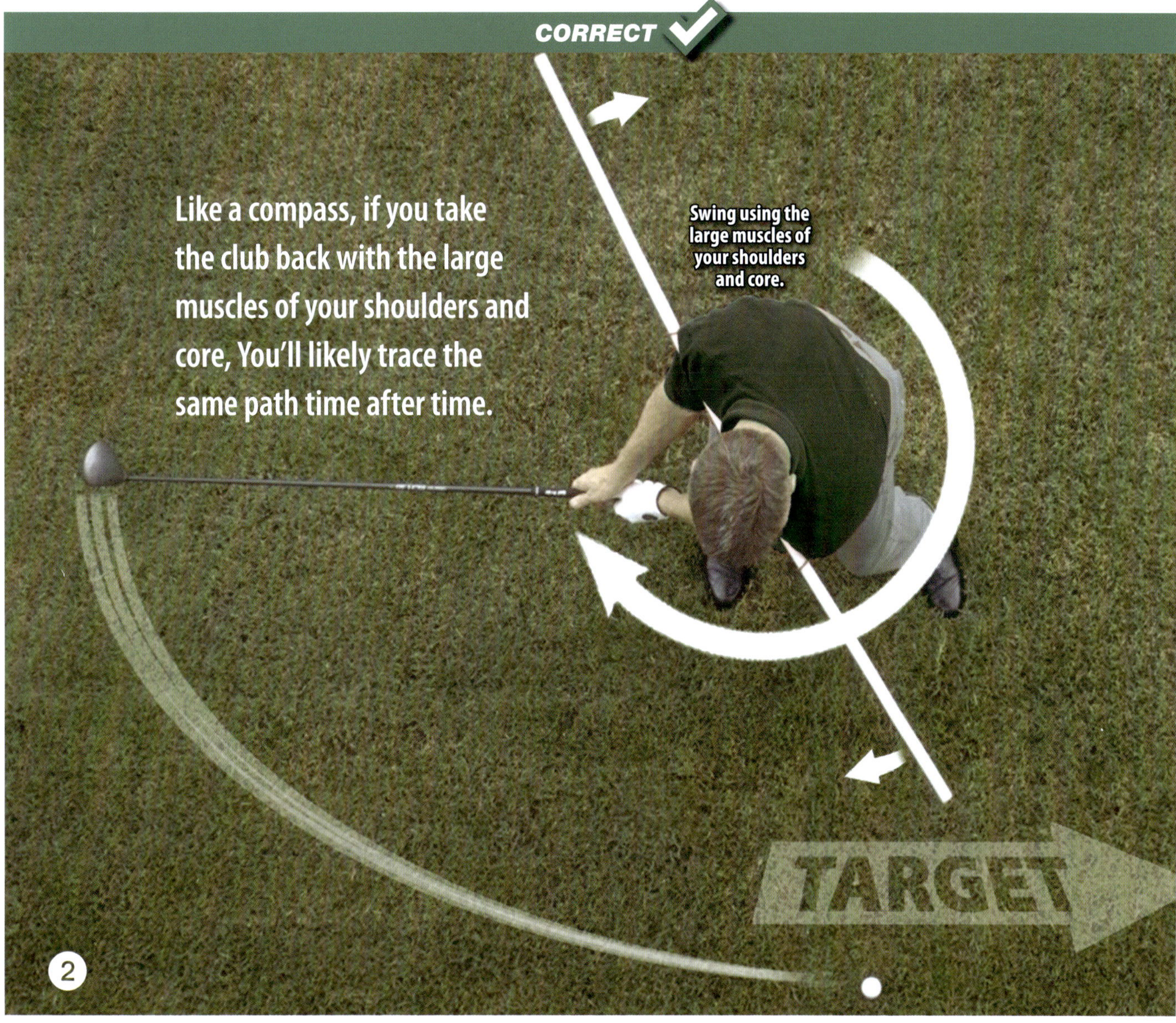

manner will allow you to swing with less effort, giving you increased distance and (eventually) greater ball control!

"The reason for practicing baseball swings before actual golf swings is important," says Don. "When my students begin swinging at an object again (the ball), they tend to revert to old habits and use their arms and hands to swing the club, just as they tended to do with their old swings. Remember what you learned when you pinched your thumbs against your forefingers? If you don't, I recommend you look back at page 76 to refresh your memory. Then, never forget it. You learned that using your hands puts tension in your longer muscles and impedes the freedom of your shoulders and torso to generate power. Let your arms swing freely – more naturally. This freedom is a product and result of the torso motions you've diligently practiced. Allow your arms and club to swing with the turning of your torso. In short: 'Be the pen and the rubber band.'"

Now that we're getting ready to begin swinging and hitting balls, make sure that you understand how to start your swing. Throughout this book you have practiced a range of movements designed to help you learn to swing efficiently. All will be in vain if you do not practice and understand how to start your swing.

"How you start your swing is the most crucial of movements," says Don. "My students will ask if they should use their lead hand, shoulders, a unified pushing motion, or some kind of pulling motion. A pulling motion that uses the muscle movement learned in the Heavy Weight Drill is the answer."

How do you fire those muscles into action? Don likes to use an analogy to provide the answer. "Let's say you were trying to move a heavy object from a shelf. You could reach out and pull the object toward you with your arms. But that would risk injury because when the shelf no longer supports the weight of the object, your arms and hands take over. This would not be a good idea with a heavy object and it is not a good idea for your golf swing."

As ❶ indicates, reaching for a heavy weight with only the arms is inefficient use the body's muscles and could result in dropping the object. In ❷, the body is closer to the heavy object allowing the load to be distributed evenly. This is not new. We do it with many everyday activities.

For example, pull-starting a lawn mower exclusively with the muscles of an arm and shoulder, creates unnecessary strain. That's why you instinctively shift your weight and lean back when you pull the cord. Using your body's core and larger muscles, including your legs, helps you accomplish the task with greater ease and efficiency.

By concentrating on, and distributing the task throughout the body, each muscle has less to do than if you assigned the task to one muscle or one group of muscles.

"You've heard the old axiom about there being strength in numbers. Well, there is strength, power, and distance in a golf swing that efficiently utilizes the largest number of muscles possible and the right ones for accomplishing the task," Don says. "When I refer to more muscles, you may envision great force or excessive energy. But, this isn't what happens. By concentrating on, and distributing the task throughout the body, each muscle has less to do than if you assigned the task to one muscle or one group of muscles."

Muscle use and muscle sequence are the keys. Concentrate on taking the club back and forth correctly and using the momentum of your weight transfer, just as you learned in the Punch Bowl Drill. And remember, a more suitable name for the so-called "one-piece take-away" should be the "every-piece take-away."

The Wrist: Just Relax

DRILL 34
THE PAINT BRUSH TAKE-AWAY

To execute the take-away properly, think of holding a paintbrush and use a similar stroking motion to 'drag' the club back.

Your wrists should be relaxed and may even break backward slightly as the club moves away from the ball. (This breaking of the wrists is OK in practice, but less so when actually hitting a ball.) If you train your hands and wrists to respond to motion instead of initiating it, your wrists won't break when you start the take-away.

DRILL 34 THE PAINT BRUSH TAKE-AWAY ▲

"I've corrected many backswings by having students concentrate on leaving the club, clubhead, and their arms just sitting there while their body or torso begins the backswing," says Don. "One of the best ways to relax the wrist and hand muscles during the backswing is what I've dubbed the 'paint brush technique.' I use this visual key for the student with a handsy or "wristy" backswing – the kind of golfer who moves the clubhead two or three feet away from the ball with her hands and arms before any of their other body parts begin to move."

During the backswing, let your arms and hands do what they also do on the through-swing – extend. With proper use of the torso during your swing, centrifugal force will take over during the downswing, pulling your arms and club extending them fully. "I always prefer arm extension over arm lift," says Don. "In fact, in most cases I try to eliminate arm lifting. Arm swinging is fine. But arm muscles should be used only to extend the arms to maintain a proper radius. The arms should be moved primarily by rotating the shoulders, back, and torso."

Width and extension on the backswing causes width and extension during the through-swing.

A narrow, restricted backswing promotes a narrow, restricted through-swing.

Chapter 9

Alignment and Aim

SWINGING FOR THE ROUGH HELPS YOU HIT STRAIGHT

Now that you've learned the motion required for a good swing and the hand positions for a good grip, it's time to learn to align your body. By positioning your feet, knees, hips, shoulders, and eyes correctly, you help ensure a centrifugal release, and your ball flight is accurate.

"This chapter includes the nine Ball-Flight Laws. These are laws, not secrets. They will help you understand the effects that the swing path and clubface have on the spin and flight of a golf ball," says Don. A spinning golf ball reacts the same as balls in other popular sports – be it soccer, bowling, baseball, or ping pong. Left-to-right spin makes the ball curve right, and right-to-left spin makes the ball curve left."

These are laws, not secrets, that will help you understand the effects the swing path and clubface have on the spin and flight of a golf ball.

It may be obvious by looking at these photos which paths and face angles are desirable. Many teachers and students would agree that a square path and a square clubface is what we all strive for. But is it?

"In my research with the Sportech Computer Golf Swing Analyzer, I determined that the swings of most professionals and low handicap players range between 1° and 7° inside-out," says Don. "This swing path automatically imparts a right-to-left spin on the ball for right-handed golfers, requiring that the face of the club be proportionately open at impact to avoid hooking the ball left of the target. This information may shed new light on your previous thinking about the golf swing. In fact, this information may very well be contradictory to what you've previously been taught – to square the club to your target at impact with the ball."

Probable outcome

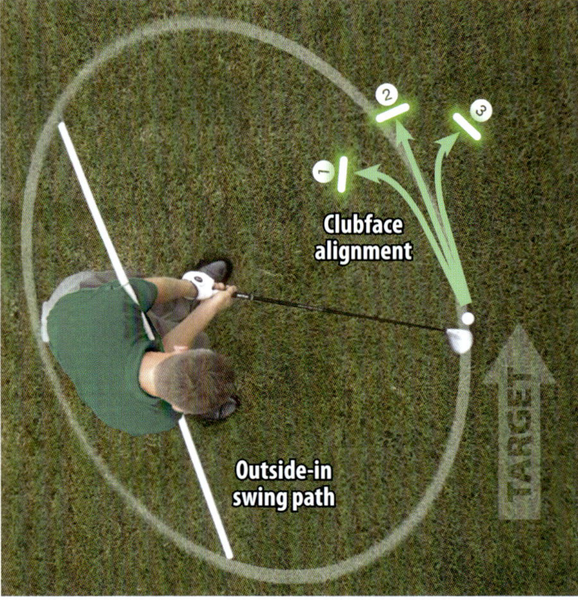

❶ PULL HOOK
❷ PULL
❸ SLICE

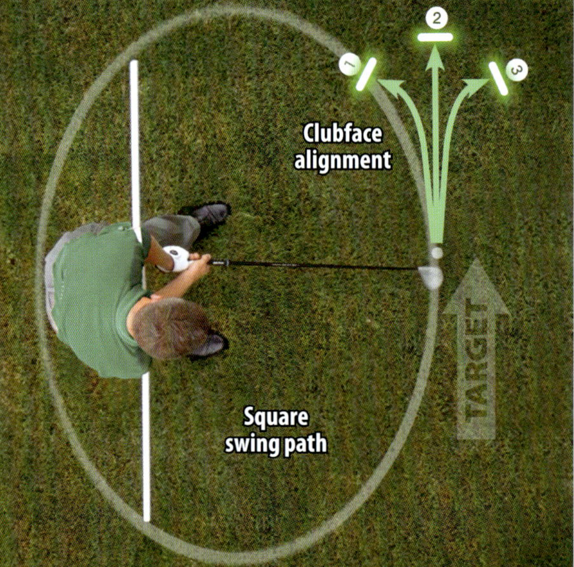

❶ DRAW
❷ STRAIGHT
❸ FADE

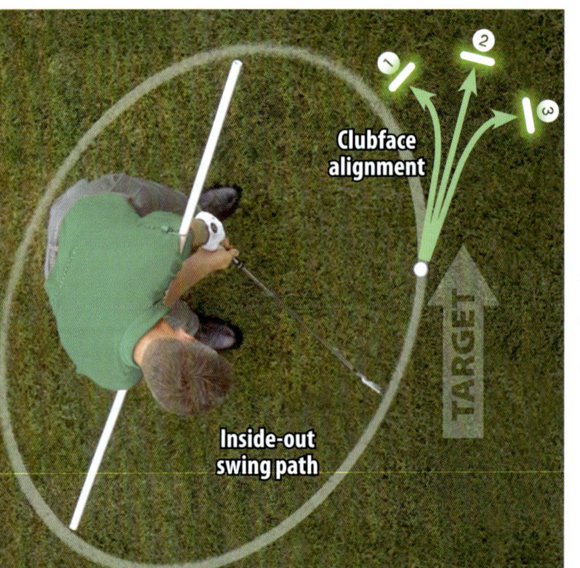

❶ HOOK
❷ PUSH
❸ PUSH SLICE

The centrifugal swinging of the clubhead will change your palm from facing up to facing the target at impact.

If even thinking of allowing the clubface to come into contact with the ball while in an open position seems counter-intuitive, it's probably because you're swinging outside-in and imparting left-to-right spin on the ball (for a right-hand golfer). This causes a slice. To hit an acceptable shot with an outside-in swing, you must exert extra effort to square the clubface. If you successfully work your way through this book, you will be able to create the inside-out swing path necessary to break out of your poor, older habits and begin grooving new, correct ones. Many good players, once they have developed an inside-out clubhead path, describe the feeling of the trail palm coming into or through the impact area in a "palm up" position.

This position may feel more familiar to you if you try it with a baseball bat. Since the baseball bat is round, there is no need to square the bat as it swings forward into the impact zone. The feeling of leaving the bat back with your trail elbow tucked in is a naturally occurring feeling in baseball. This sensation feels wrong in golf.

"Professional players swing inside-out, imparting desirable right-to-left spin on the ball. The clubface does not need to be physically manipulated by the smaller muscles into a closed or even square position at impact," says Don. "The accomplished player's clubface will close naturally due to the centrifugal force created by the swing and natural pull of the body by its core. In a way it's like trusting your body core to be the sun and your clubhead a distant planet. The planet can travel to the far reaches of the solar system, but forces draw it back toward the system's center. To create the desired inside-out swing, proper alignment and aim is required.

"If you want something cosmic going on in your swing, there you have it. It's no great mystery. To create your good inside-out swing, let's review some simple laws of science that were first introduced to you in grade school."

SWING **NOTE!** ***Self-squaring clubhead.***

A slightly inside-out path, along with a slightly open face, contacts the inside quadrant of the ball at impact. In the fraction of a second when the ball is on the clubface, centrifugal force squares the clubface and the ball is propelled toward the target.

An inside-out swing path together with an open face at impact...

...results in a square face at launch!

The two major alignment problems are misalignment of the feet and misalignment of the shoulders. Aligning the feet properly is easy to practice. Simply take a club, a rake, or any other straight stick, place it on the ground in front of you, and align it parallel to your intended target line.

Aligning your shoulders properly takes a little more practice. The most common mistake is allowing your lead hand closer to the body than the trail hand, which is positioned lower on the grip. (In learning golf, most people are taught to put the lead hand at the top of the grip and keep the arm straight.)

Most of us have two arms that are the same length (❸). If your lead arm is straight, it is physically impossible to place your trail hand below your lead hand and keep it straight without unwittingly shifting your shoulder alignment away from parallel. In reaching out with the trail hand, there is a tendency to shift the trail shoulder out to place it below the lead hand (❶). You can see how the shoulders shift incorrectly and cause the body to open slightly to the target.

Try this instead: Lower your trail shoulder and raise your lead shoulder so that both remain square to the intended target (❷). Perform this movement as comfortably without disturbing your lower body. This adjustment will cause your lead shoulder to tilt higher than the trail shoulder (❹).

"There may or may not be a conscious sliding or placing of the hips forward. Be aware that the spine angle is altered up to 7° when great players lower their trail shoulder to set up to the ball," says Don.

When gripping a club, you may initially feel uncomfortable aligning your shoulders correctly. Don offers this tip to correct the problem. Start with your lead hand on the club and your trail hand hanging at your side. Reach down low enough to feel as if you are reaching up to the grip.

"In other words," says Don, "reach lower at first, and then come back up by bending or breaking your trail elbow joint slightly."

Lowering the trail shoulder creates the ideal posture – head a bit behind the ball, hips slightly forward, and a spine angle tilted slightly over the trail hip.

As a golf instructor, Don likes to find new ways to exaggerate correct positions and motions to help his students understand swing concepts.

A Try holding a basketball or a beach ball with your hands on either side.

B Turn the ball away from your target placing your trail hand and shoulder at the bottom, your lead hand and shoulder on top. This motion emphasizes the feeling you should have in your shoulders when you properly address the ball.

THE ROLE OF DEPTH IN THE SWING

Many golfers who slice, fade, or shank do not create enough depth in their golf swing to attack the ball from the inside. Golf swing depth is how far inside (in relation to the ball) your hands travel during your backswing. It is important to create depth in your swing. It is the role of the shoulders to do so. The more depth in your backswing, the easier it will be for you to swing inside-out on your through-swing. Conversely, the less depth in your backswing, the harder it will be to swing on an inside-out path.

If you feel depth is a problem in your swing, go back and practice your shoulder turn with a broom handle (Chapter 5). If your lead shoulder is not turning behind the ball, you are not creating enough depth to swing the club on an inside-out path during your downswing.

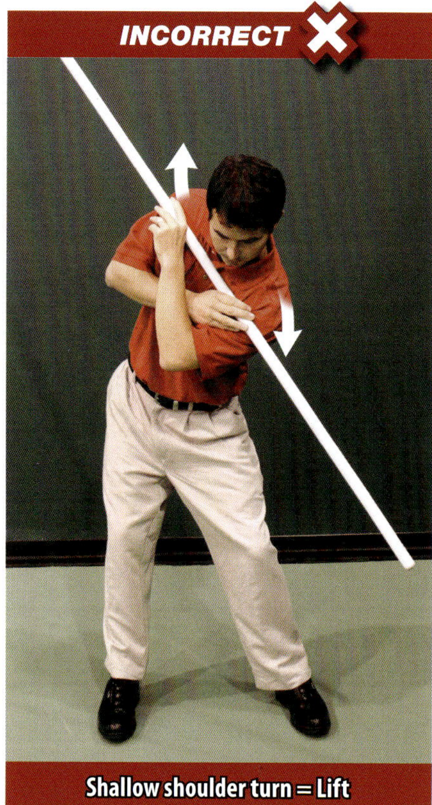

Shallow shoulder turn = Lift

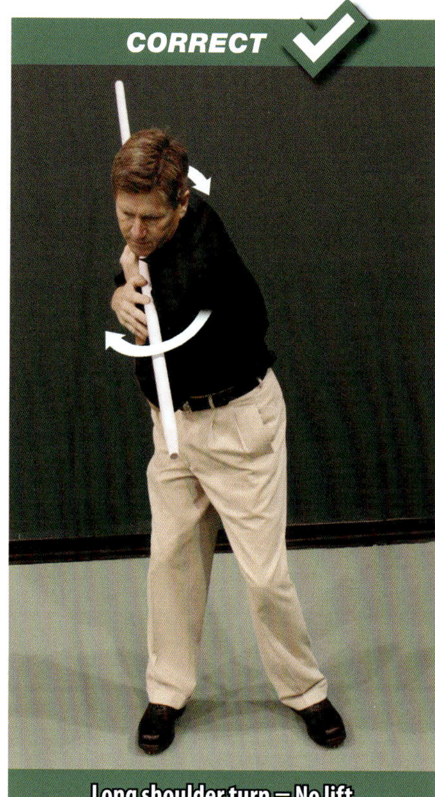

Long shoulder turn = No lift

FORGET TIMING

"I can't begin to recall how many times I've heard teachers blame timing as the culprit for their students' poor golf shots. 'Just work on your timing, and your hitting will be fine,' they say. In my opinion, timing isn't something you want to work on, but something you want to eliminate. Do you realize that at the instant of impact an average player's swing generates up to 2,000 pounds of force? That's a ton! Trying to consistently control a clubhead that possesses that much force using only the small muscles of your hands and arms is an impossible task!"

Think back to the example of the record player (page 63) when you pictured a coin on the outside edge of a record. It doesn't matter that we live in high-tech digital age. The golf swing has roots that go even farther back than a record player. Remember that when we repeated the process the same way each time, the record player cast a coin off the record at the same place every time. This didn't occur because of timing on the record player's part. It occurred because of a repeatable sequence of events and the laws of centrifugal force and inertia. The same concept applies to the Sidearm Throwing Drill (page 64). If your motion follows the correct sequence, the ball is released at the same point every time.

THINK SEQUENCE

Your body is made up of many different muscle groups, all capable of working separately. Training your muscles correctly requires an understanding of sequence. Picture five race cars headed independently toward a finish line. The yellow car represents your clubhead. Moving across the track, the green car is your trail shoulder and arm. The blue car carries the hands which are joined together at the grip. The purple car represents your hips and the red car represents your lead shoulder and arm.

Imagine how difficult it would be to "time" all these cars to cross the finish line at precisely the same moment. All have different engines and drivers. The drivers all have different driving tendencies and habits. Picture the finish line as the golf ball. Rather than winning the race, the goal is to cross the finish line at top speed in unison. How often might these different cars and drivers be able to accomplish that goal at anything approaching top speed? The answer is not very often. Yet, that is what the average golfer attempts when he or she relies on timing rather than sequence to square the clubface at impact.

Timing is not something you want to work on, but something you want to eliminate.

The individual cars of the train represent your hips, shoulders, arms, hands, and clubhead. The train is an express train speeding down a track. It is headed for the end of the line – that wonderful place where the club rests on your lead shoulder as you admire your shot soaring down the middle of the fairway.

The ball in this scenario is a stop along the way to the end of the line. The different cars roar through that stop at top speed in perfect position and sequence every time. Each car powerfully follows the next combining greater force at impact.

"Professional golfers possess superb sequencing that results in great golf shots. They know that if they start their backswings and downswings correctly, the rest is taken care of," says Don. "When the sequence of motion in your swing is carried out correctly, and you start with correct alignment, everything else will fall into place. You can forget about timing."

Five race cars representing five key muscle groups ~~have the goal~~ [try] to cross the finish line at top speed in unison.

This is *very* difficult to accomplish when relying on timing rather than sequence to square the clubface at impact.

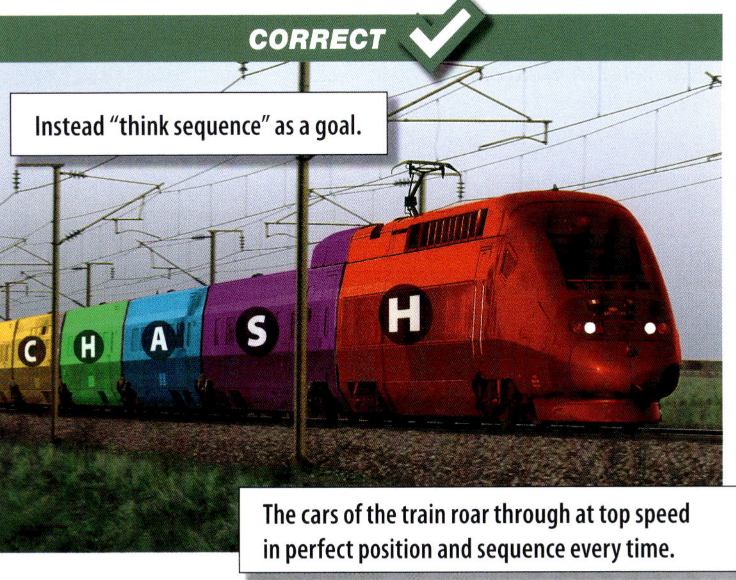

Instead "think sequence" as a goal.

The cars of the train roar through at top speed in perfect position and sequence every time.

Impact

DRILL 35 TEETER-TOTTER DRILL ▶

"This exercise identifies the precise manner for changing the direction of your swing from backswing to downswing, the most difficult aspect of the golf swing to learn," says Don. "Efficient change of direction truly separates professionals from amateurs, better players from lesser players, and long hitters from short hitters. The more quickly players transfer their weight (without sacrificing efficiency), the farther they hit the ball."

Keep your body parts connected during this drill so your shoulders, torso, and the club rotate only slightly. Do not swing your arms forward, except to the extent that they move due to the slight torso rotation caused by the "teeter-totter" motion. The club action here is similar to a batter 'checking' a baseball swing. Keep your trail arm resting against your rib cage as you oscillate. Focus on your heels as you move your weight back and forth.

This drill will help you develop a smooth change of direction in your swing.

Cock your wrists so the club is parallel to the ground and aligned along the target line.

Heel up

Heel down

REPEAT THE ENTIRE DRILL 10 TIMES, CONTINUING TO SHIFT YOUR WEIGHT BACK AND FORTH.

Using the "punch bowl away" verbal cue, rotate your torso and club away from the target. Like a teeter-totter, oscillate back and forth between these two positions.

Focus primarily on the up-and-down movement of your heels (shift back and forth) while the club moves up and down. Don't just lift the lead heel. Let the torque created by turning your shoulders pull it slightly off the ground. Make sure your hands and wrists don't release as you move toward the target and onto your lead foot – just like a checked swing in baseball.

SWING NOTE! *Swing rpms.*

The Teeter-Totter Drill and upcoming Windshield Wiper and Opposite Field drills all promote the "marriage" of your hips and hands. To execute your best swing, your hands and hips should move consistently through impact at the same revolutions per minute just as with the carousel analogy (page 32).

DRILL 36 WINDSHIELD WIPER DRILL ▼

As you have learned in this book, hitting a baseball requires a horizontal plane or near-horizontal swing plane. However, hitting a golf ball off the ground requires you to swing on an inclined plane. As a result, the club must move up and in during the backswing and down and out during the downswing. These pages offer two views of a proper release and a clear understanding of how the club approaches the ball at impact. A-C show the clubhead

Impact

DRILL 36

WINDSHIELD WIPER DRILL

This drill helps train your hands and wrists for a correct release and establishes the bottom of your swing arc for precise ball striking.

Begin by repeating the Teeter-Totter Drill and hold the finish position (A and A) with your weight firmly established on your lead leg, hips slightly open, and your trail knee pointing in. Your trail heel is slightly off the ground. Align the club shaft parallel with your feet making sure your hips are open, but your shoulders and chest remain parallel (or square) with your feet and the club shaft. While moving no body parts other than your wrists, unhinge them and allow the club to swing down and out to the ground. Make sure your hands are positioned slightly ahead of the shaft and clubhead (B and B) and your lead wrist does not cup as you unhinge. Also note that the clubface appears slightly open to the target at the point where it begins to brush the ground. You can even stop your swing at this point and note the position of the club.

As the clubhead continues past this point (impact), turn your hips, chest and shoulders just enough (without moving your wrists) for the clubhead to extend 10 or 12 inches past the impact point (C and C). Once you have observed these three positions, return the club to the starting position and repeat the motion several times. Increase the briskness of the motion, just as you would increase the speed of wipers on a windshield as a light rain begins to fall harder.

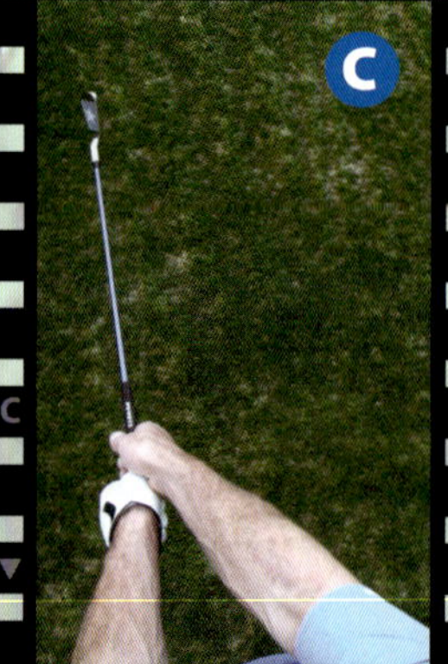

moving down toward the bottom of the swing arc. A-C show a golfer's view of the clubhead moving toward the outermost point of the swing arc – called the apex.

Don't cup the lead wrist.

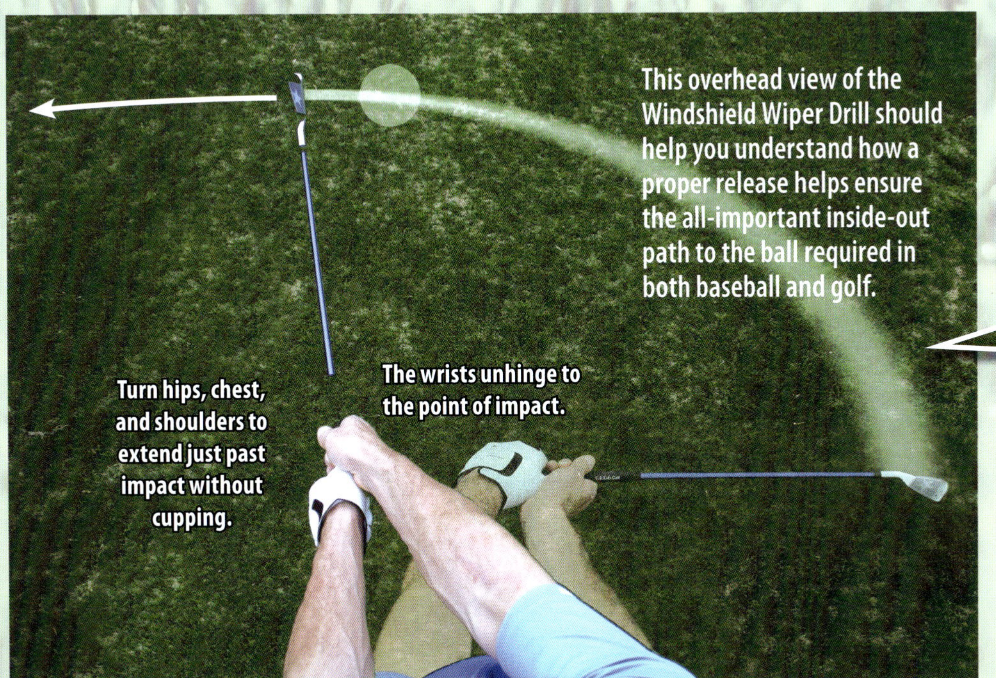

VISUALIZATION

As you continue to practice the Windshield Wiper Drill, it might be helpful to visualize a clock face on a ball. For purposes of the upcoming drills, imagine the ball sitting on home plate of a baseball field ❶. Approach the golf ball from the inside toward a point represented by 7 o'clock. Many golfers and teachers embrace this image of feeling the clubhead traveling from inside-to-out on a 7 to 1 o'clock path. Therefore, proper ball position is almost precisely at the point where the clubhead reaches the bottom and outermost point of the swing arc. We'll talk more about ball position later. For now, let's use the clock image to help us swing the club with confidence, attack the inside of the ball, feel centrifugal force, and develop the release you need to be a better golfer.

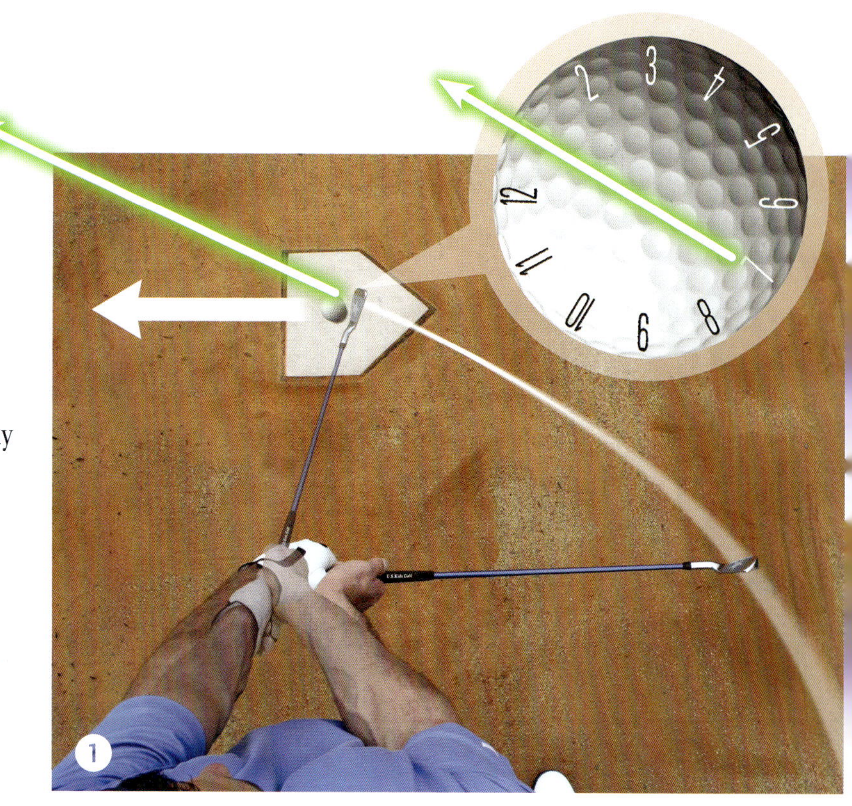

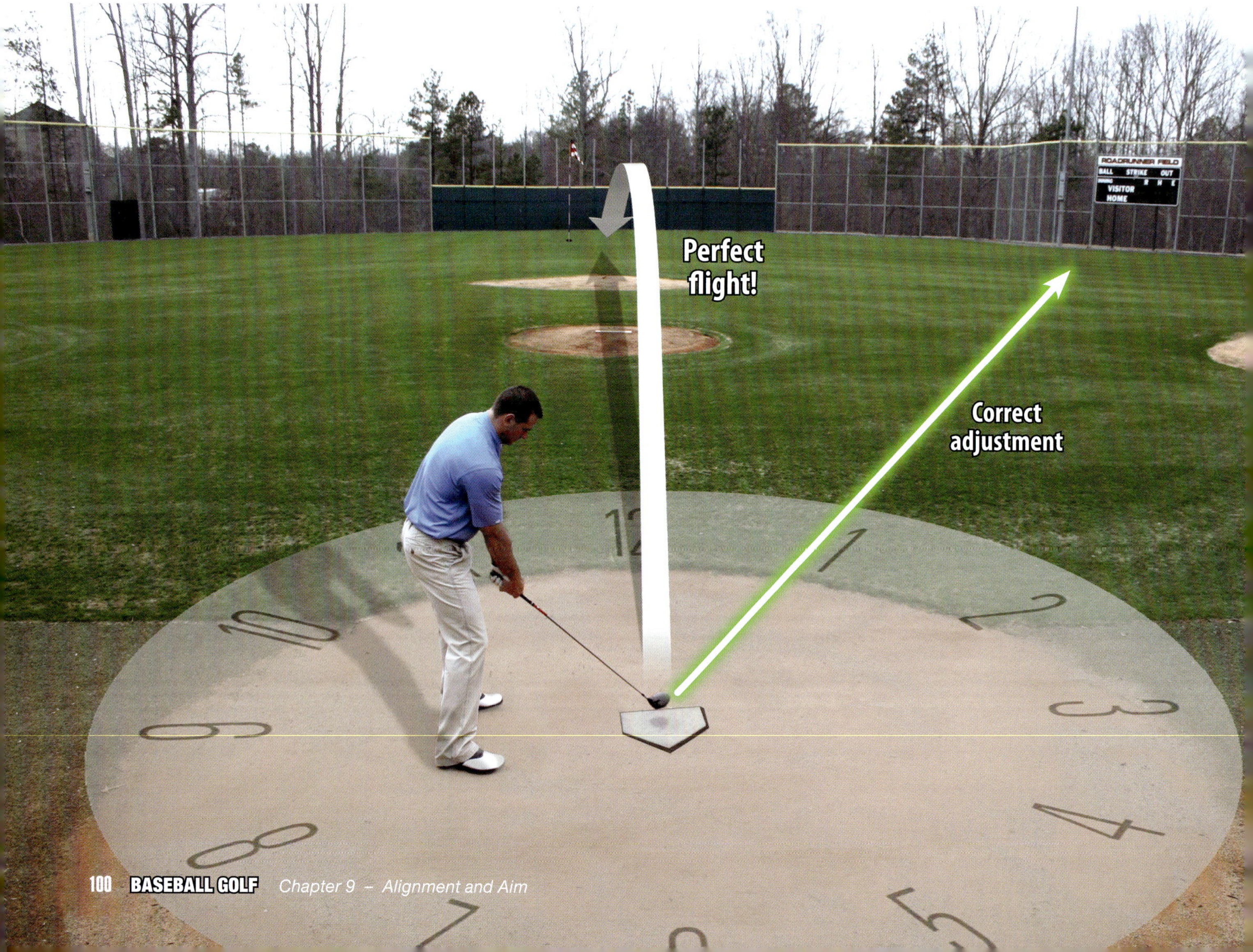

Perfect flight!

Correct adjustment

THINK OPPOSITE FIELD!

One of the key concepts of the *Baseball Golf* swing is to think opposite field when you swing a golf club, eventually taking this simple thought to the range and even the golf course. Imagine that you are standing at home plate. Allow your imagination to superimpose the image of a baseball field before you. The Teeter-Totter with the Windshield Wiper drills should have given you a sense of throwing the clubhead toward the opposite field. After all, the clubhead is moving in that direction throughout much of the downswing to the bottom of the swing where it begins to flip over and square to the target. As it flips and squares, the clubhead maintains an arc along a tilted plane and launches the ball on its way. All this happens so fast that you will still be thinking about swinging toward the opposite field after the ball is on its way to centerfield – also known as the middle of the fairway.

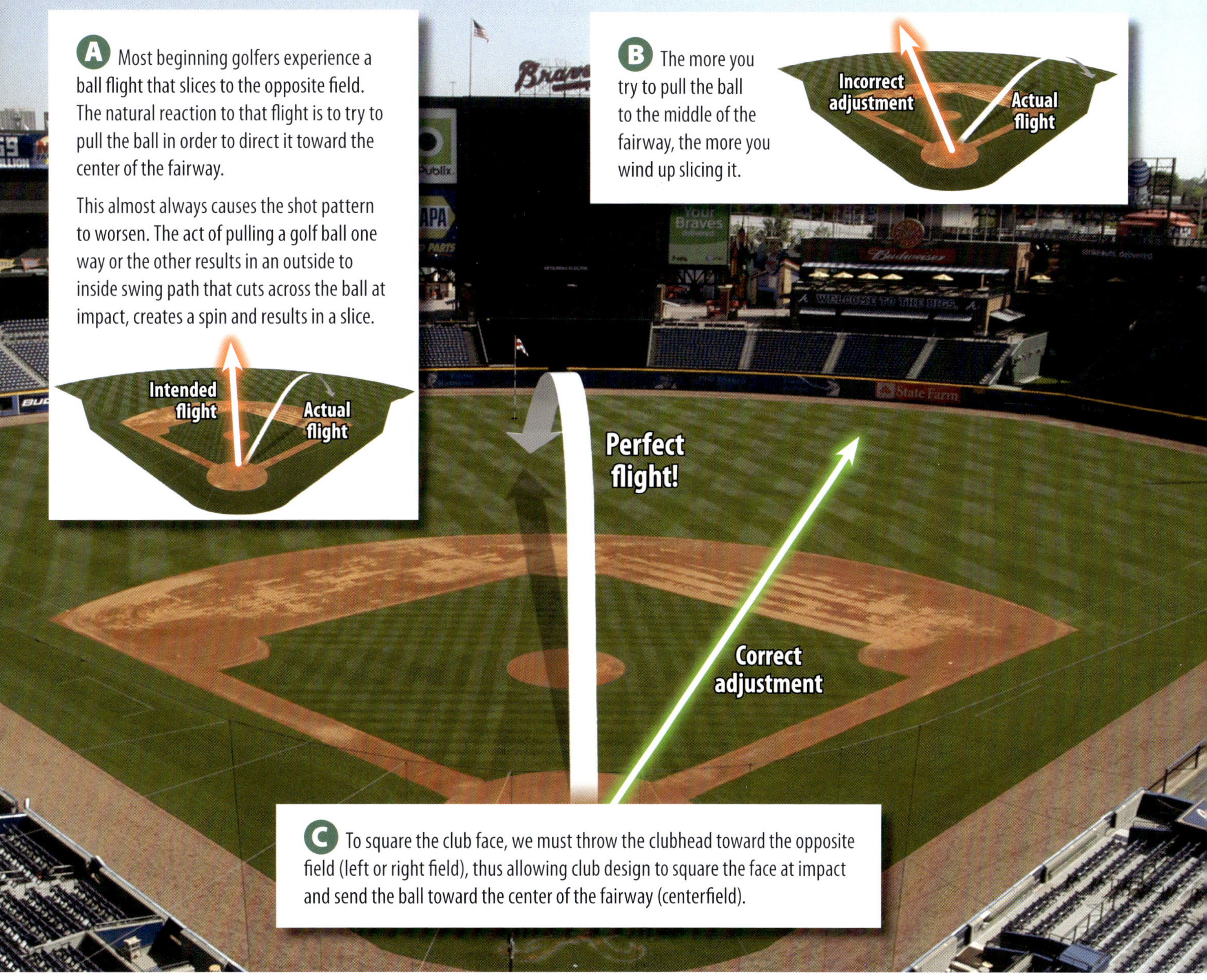

Thinking opposite field seems like such a simple concept. Why then is execution so difficult? The answer is rather obvious. Centerfield is the fairway.

The act of fearlessly releasing the club toward either the left side (for the left-handed golfer) or right side of the fairway (for the right-handed golfer) seems counter-intuitive. But, it works. It is simply a matter of trusting club design and letting go of your swing fears.

DRILL 37 OPPOSITE FIELD DRILL

The opposite field drill is a pre-set drill designed to help you feel and understand a proper release of your hands, wrists, and the clubhead through the impact area.

The Opposite Field Drill is simply the Teeter-Totter Drill and the Windshield Wiper Drill with a follow-through. Follow along closely and pay special attention to every detail of this drill. Maximum benefits require correct execution.

SETUP

TEETER-TOTTER MOTION

from the Teeter-totter Drill (page 96)

With wrists hinged and the club shaft parallel with the ground (above) and parallel with your feet (below)...

A ...begin the teeter-totter motion without moving a muscle in your arms, hands, or wrists.

REPEAT THIS SEGMENT THREE TIMES.

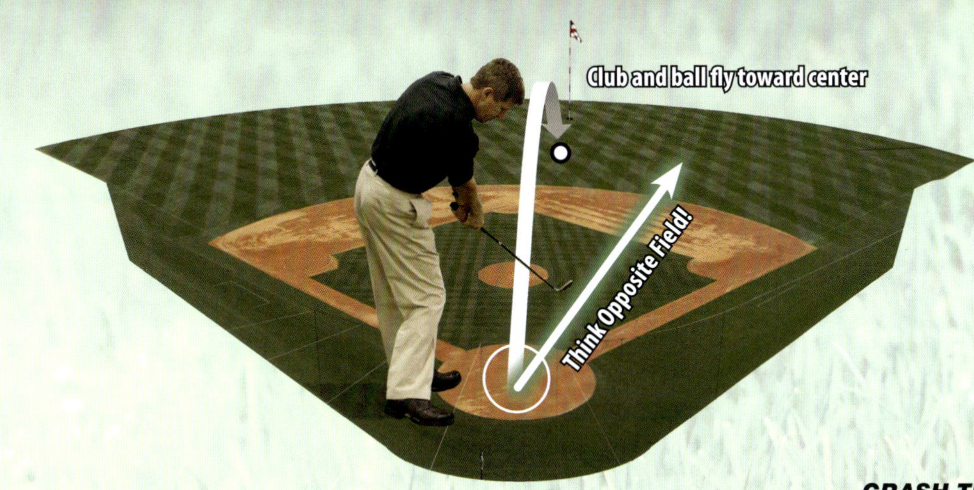

IMPACT

WINDSHIELD WIPER RELEASE

CRASH THE CYMBALS FOLLOW-THROUGH

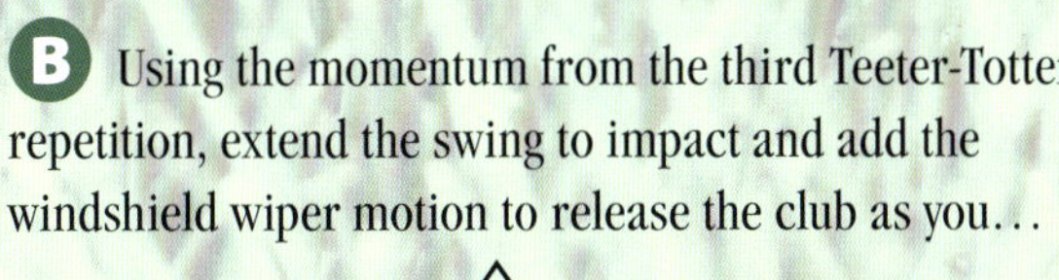

B Using the momentum from the third Teeter-Totter repetition, extend the swing to impact and add the windshield wiper motion to release the club as you…

C …Crash the Cymbals while swinging to the opposite field. Allow the club to release as the clubhead turns over to point skyward, the shaft is down the target line toward what would be center field in baseball.

Using What You've Learned

HIP SLIDE DRILL

"Bump" your hips toward the target to initiate your downswing.

TEE BALL DRILL

Smash the ball with your hips...

DRILL 38 DOWNSWING FUSION DRILL ▲

Downswing fusion is the yang to the backswing yin. Your downswing sets in motion forces that uncoil the body and release the club through the ball to your proper, tall finish.

With a proper backswing, the downswing becomes almost involuntary. The body simply snaps back as the bow and arrow or a slingshot does. "I encourage my students to be aggressive with their turn-through motion, but try to repeat it the same way every time," says Don. "Hogan once commented that the harder he swung, the straighter he hit it."

"Remember, swing hard with your hips and everything else will follow. It's like a tractor with a bunch of wagons hooked up behind it. If all the wagons were in a crooked line, what would happen if you started the tractor and began driving in a straight line? It may take a few seconds, but those wagons would also be pulled into a straight line. That's precisely what can happen in your golf swing if you allow your hips to be the tractor, and your shoulders, arms, and club to be the wagons."

CRASH THE CYMBALS DRILL

...to help you spring through...

TURN UP DRILL

...for a balanced finish.

SWING NOTE! *Feel The Target.*

There is a famous highlight of NBA star Larry Bird running to save a ball which is headed out of bounds in the corner of the court some 50 feet from the goal (his target). Looking away from the basket, Bird grabs the ball, heaves a high arcing shot over his shoulder straight into the basket. Lucky, you say. "Maybe not just lucky," says Don. "You see, Bird had been on that court many times practicing for many hours. He had learned everything to know about his environment. His instincts knew exactly where the target was and his mind told his body how to get the ball to go there.

There are also stories of sharp shooters who can shoot clay pigeons and coins thrown into the air by shooting from the hip – without using the gun's sight.

The best golfers do the same thing. Even though golf courses are different, all have similar targets – fairways, greens and holes. Great golfers develop a feel for their environment as well. Try this mental exercise. Pretend you are putting, but you are blind. The hole has a device that beeps to help you know where to aim. Since you cannot visually aim to make the ball go toward the hole, use your other senses to align toward the hole (target) or where you feel your body should send the ball.

Let's take a look at some of the key motions you've learned to construct your new Baseball Golf swing.

These motions are your new best friends. Continue to practice with them from time to time to keep your swing in shape.

If you take time away from the game or begin to swing poorly, revisit each drill and train as you did the first time you read through this book. It will amaze you how repeating the correct motions a few times using one of these simple drills can dramatically affect your swing.

"I will always remember the golf school where I introduced some of my training drills for the first time," says Don. "I rushed through the Heavy Weight, Punch Bowl, and Tee Ball drills because I felt the students might find them rather insignificant or boring. After the half-day class, I decided to buy everyone a Coke and ask for some feedback. To my pleasure and amazement, every student thought we should have spent more time on the drills. They recognized the value of this type of training, just as I always have."

It will amaze you how repeating the correct motions a few times using one of these simple drills can dramatically affect your swing.

Putting It All Together

DRILL 39
FINAL FUSION DRILL

Final Fusion is as much a mental exercise as it is a physical drill to help you fuse all the intricate motions of the Baseball Golf drills together with the aid of a total swing thought.

Simply combine the motions of the (A) Backswing Fusion Drill (page 56) and the (B) Downswing Fusion Drill (page 104). The former instructed you how to "stretch back" and the latter how to "spring through." Perform each drill again. Then, while reflecting on the visual message of the bow and arrow image (page 55), fuse the instructions mentioned above into your Baseball Golf total swing thought: "Stretch Back and Spring Through."

To powerfully coil and uncoil, cue yourself by thinking: "Stretch Back and Spring Through."

DRILL 39 FINAL FUSION DRILL ▲

The Final Fusion Drill helps you fuse all the motions of the Baseball Golf Windup and Delivery drills into simple motions of swinging back and swinging through. Together your backswing and downswing help you complete the circular/centrifugal motion of your golf swing. They combine to let you release the club and follow through to a tall, full finish.

To make the Final Fusion easier, it is best to simplify your swing thoughts. As you recall at the start of this book, we talked about how too many confusing and conflicting swing thoughts make it difficult to execute an athletic golf swing.

Breaking down the golf swing into smaller, easier to learn pieces made it possible for you to focus on one part of the swing at a time, using one or two verbal/mental cues. As you progressed with each drill, we layered each part of the swing sequence onto your knowledge base. Now your mind and body know how to swing. You just have to mentally get out of the way and let that happen.

"I think the best way to accomplish this can be summed up in two phrases, 'Stretch back' and 'Spring through'. These simple phrases embody all the actions of the foundation-building drills and fuse them together into a well-constructed and reliable swing. I like these phrases because they seem to conjure up more of a coiling and uncoiling image. They are also easy to remember," says Don.

At this point you're almost ready to walk to the tee, point your body toward the target and fire balls at the pin – like arrows from a bow.

We are now a single drill away from a series of training routines in which you will begin hitting golf balls! This drill and the training sequence that follows it are designed to help train your mind to keep your arms and hands relaxed and the club in proper position. Then you can strike the ball with confidence, precision and maximum power. This is what you want in a golf swing. You will attain these capabilities if you remain patient just a little bit longer.

Chapter 10

The "Big Picture"

DIRECT THE BALL BETTER BY FOCUSING ON IT LESS

Now that you're ready to put a golf ball in the way of your new swing, let's talk about how you should look at the ball.

As a result of years of well-intended tips and magazine articles, it is common to stand over the ball and wonder about a variety of things such as: "Do I aim at the whole ball? Do I aim at a dimple? Do I aim at part of the ball and, if so, what part of the ball am I trying to hit?" The list goes on.

"The problem with these questions is they all focus too much on the ball," says Don. "If you over-focus on the ball, you're missing the big picture. In golf you have to look at the big picture, just like you consider more than the road when you're driving a car. In order to drive the ball and avoid obstacles such as water, sand, rough, and the woods, you must embrace the same mentality that allows you to avoid such obstacles as pedestrians, lampposts, and other vehicles. Remember your driver education instructor advising you to be aware of everything happening around you – oncoming traffic, upcoming traffic signals, kids playing alongside the road, dogs chasing cats, etc. It's important to do the same thing in golf."

Take in the whole picture, of which the ball is one very small part. Pay attention to your target, the shape of the shot you're attempting, where the wind is coming from, the alignment of your feet, and the alignment of your shoulders.

"Seeing the big picture allows you to focus on your target and what you have to do to get the ball to go there," says Don. "Staring at a single dimple of the golf ball tends to freeze your mind, stiffen your grip, and keep you from swinging freely for the target."

If you tend to over-focus on the ball at address, try

taking a visual inventory of everything around you while using your peripheral vision and quick glances to check the alignment of your feet, shoulders, and the clubface. Don't ignore the target. Even if you've chosen a spot just ahead of the ball, along your target line as a reference or aiming point, look up at the target... relax... maybe even take a deep breath.

Seeing the big picture allows you to focus on your target and what you have to do to get the ball to go there.

"Taking a visual inventory of all these things will help prevent you from focusing too much on the ball," says Don. "The big picture includes maintaining a picture of the target in your mind's eye, even while you are looking at the ball. A golfer whose focus is too much on the ball is mentally out of balance. And being mentally out balance in golf is likely to produce a swing that's physically out of balance. Balance is about both the mind and the body. You must work on training your mind to be aware of all these things in order to be in total balance."

So now we're ready to hit the golf course, right? We've practiced a bunch of drills. We see the big picture. We're are ready to be the pen and the rubber band. We're ready to hit great golf shots, because all that's missing is a ball to place in the way of the clubhead as it hurtles with speed and power along the path of our new and improved golf swing. Right?

Not quite. There is one element we haven't added, or more properly stated, haven't removed yet: shedding the last remnants of our old golf swing and using a new and improved *Baseball Golf* swing.

Most golf professionals can "catch" a ball as easily as Tiger did in his famous commercial, where he showed us his ability to bounce the ball on the face of his sand wedge.

Baseball players, even 3-year-olds, routinely "catch" the ball with their bats – even though the ball is moving!

As long as it's within reach, baseball players easily "catch" the ball whether high or low.

Tennis players routinely "catch" the tennis ball in the center of the tennis racket.

You may have been able to hit the ball fairly solidly with your old swing, but it likely felt different than your new one. If you have made changes in your swing as you have worked through this book, even minor ones, then you must acquire a completely new feel and learn to hit the middle of the ball in the middle of the clubhead with that new feel.

"If you're a beginner, you'll need to spend some time developing *eye-clubhead coordination*," says Don. "If this term sounds familiar, it is. It's a phrase I coined as a take-off on eye-hand coordination. In baseball you use eye-hand coordination to catch the ball in the glove hand. In golf we use our eyes and an extension of our hands (the club) to 'catch' the ball with the clubhead, which is at the end of a whippy shaft. I like using the word 'catch' to describe the manner in which we make contact with the ball. After all, if I were to throw you a ball that was high above your head, you would reach up to catch it. If I were to throw you a ball that was low, you would instinctively reach down to catch it. That's why you must develop your eye-club coordination – so you can catch the ball solidly in the middle of the clubhead whether the ball is sitting high on the side of a hill or flat in the fairway. In different situations you will adjust your stance and spine angle slightly, but your feel for catching the ball in the middle of the clubface must be as natural as catching a ball in your glove hand."

SWING NOTE! Catch the Ball.

"Catching" the ball solidly is much easier than you think. Nearly every club designed currently copies the original Ping iron from years ago where the weight or mass of metal is distributed towards the outside of the iron creating the 'cavity back.' This design lowers the 'sweet spot' or center of mass to a point lower than most golfers realize," says Don. "Essentially, all we need to do for airborne shots is strike the center of mass of a golf ball with the center of mass of the golf club. By studying these pictures you can relax, just knowing your club doesn't need to be directed as precisely as you thought.

"Cavity Back" iron design

Most believe the sweet spot or center of mass is here.

But, because of design features it is actually here.

Mentally, it's much easier to swing centrifugally through the golf ball when you know you have a margin of error. See how far off the ground the sole of the iron is when we line up the centers of mass!

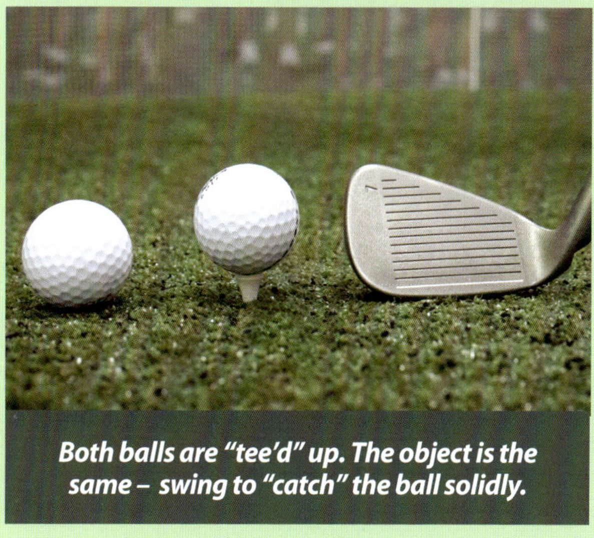
Both balls are "tee'd" up. The object is the same – swing to "catch" the ball solidly.

By now you've performed the drills as directed, and understand how they will help improve your game. Resist the urge to start hitting balls off the ground. Doing so at this point will likely lead to old bad habits and destroy the foundation you've built by using this book.

Instead, we want you to start by hitting from an elevated tee. Practicing with the ball elevated is an old golf training method that has been around for years. Originally practiced on the side of a hill, this method was developed to help golfers who swing too upright (steep). Elevating the ball to simulate a hillside will help prevent you from lifting your arms during the backswing. The same holds true for those students who tilt their shoulders, causing a steep swing angle. This old trick seems to cure many problems inherent to golf swings, regardless of your skill level. For instance, take an experience Don had with PGA tour player Tim Simpson.

"If hitting off the side of a hill can help a pro like Simpson, just think what simulating a side-hill lie can do for you."

Don was teaching at the Harbor Club in Lake Oconee, Georgia in 1998. Simpson, recovering from a bout with Lyme Disease, was struggling to find his old swing which had been one of the most reliable in golf. Once the PGA's Greens in Regulation leader, Simpson's swing was faltering badly. To compensate, he was simply aiming at the middle of the greens.

"I was the new head pro and Tim was a longstanding club member of considerable renown," says Don. "He didn't know much about my playing or teaching background, only that he hadn't heard of me."

They were introduced on the range one day, and Don hung around to watch Tim hit balls. "The rhythm of his swing was still equal to anyone in golf, but he had begun to come over the top and was having difficulty striking shots solidly with his familiar draw. Instead he was hitting a slight fade with his irons, and losing control of his drives."

After a few minutes, Simpson turned and asked Don, "What do you see?"

Don asked him a few questions to get a dialog started and then told him very directly, "You should strengthen your grip, close your stance, and hit off the side of a hill for a week." The suggestion got a cool refusal. Don hung around only briefly before retreating to the pro shop. A week later Simpson asked Don to videotape his swing so he could send a tape to Butch Harmon for analysis. Don obliged. At the time Harmon was working with

Greg Norman and a still somewhat-unknown named Tiger Woods.

A couple of weeks later on a rainy day that didn't hold much promise for play, Don was closing up the pro shop early when the phone rang. "It was Tim calling from Atlanta. He asked me if I could keep the range open because he had gotten his tape back and wanted to hit some balls. I asked him what Butch said, and Tim just laughed," recalls Don.

Simpson replied, "You aren't going to believe this, Don, but Butch said I should strengthen my grip, close my stance and hit off the side of a hill for a week! Don, I've been on tour for almost 20 years, and I'd never heard of such a thing. Within two weeks, two teaching pros told me exactly the same thing."

Simpson went to the Tour School so he could qualify for play the following year without using his medical exemption. He shot rounds of 66, 67, 66, 67, and 71 to breeze through. When he returned to the Harbor Club, Don couldn't resist ribbing him about the final round of 71. It turns out, Simpson said he hit the ball as well that day as he had the previous four.

"What happened?" asked Don.

"I fired at the middle of the greens just to play safe," said Simpson. "I hit 17 greens in regulation, had 4 birdies, and three-putted three times. I just pured it!"

Practicing with the ball elevated is an old golf training method that has been around for years. Originally practiced on the side of a hill, this method was developed to help those golfers who swing the club too upright.

The moral of this story: If hitting off the side of a hill can help a pro like Simpson, just think what simulating a side-hill lie can do for you.

"Since I began writing *Baseball Golf* back in 1987, I've seen no less than five other golf instructors exhibit some sort of elevated training device at the annual golf merchandise show in Florida," says Don. "Many teachers and players agree that this method works. It's been around for years and it is not going away."

"When I first became a full time golf instructor, I began using the side of a hill to train many students. After just a few lessons, I would run out of grass to use. That's when I developed a table that accomplished the same thing," says Don. "To help keep you on track and away from the course, I recommend setting up a hitting area in your home and practicing there before heading to the range.

If this sounds boring or overly demanding, what Don proposes requires only a couple of cardboard boxes, some couch cushion (old or new), a small carpet sample or remnant, a rubber tee, and some practice balls. If you use boxes, they should be relatively long and at least a foot wide. Heavy garment boxes work well. Long surfaces are necessary because many people hit behind or under the ball when taking their initial swings from an elevated tee. Elongated boxes or cushions will allow you to raise and then gradually lower the level of your golf ball in stages of a few inches at a time from the knees down. Assemble the items placing the piece of carpet (with a hole cut in it for the tee) or a practice mat on top of the cushions or boxes.

When practicing indoors, the first goal is safety. Don recommends using foam or whiffle practice balls, "I've even used wadded up pieces of paper when nothing else was available."

DRILL 40 *THE KNEE-HIGH SWING* ▶

"Most of my students hit the ball more solidly when they are trying to swing just over the top of the ball," says Don. "It's important to practice this until you get the feel of swinging around and around instead of up and down. In essence, you are a baseball player using a golf club held with a golfer's grip to hit a knee-high pitch. Spend at least three practice sessions working from this level while doing your Backswing and the Downswing Fusion drills.

After you've become proficient hitting inside at this level, you can either head for the range with your hitting surfaces, or continue to practice inside using plastic golf balls. The transitional training routines in the next chapter are designed to help you fully groove your new swing.

Take several baseball swings over the ball to avoid initial errant swings.

DRILL 40

THE KNEE-HIGH SWING

With the boxes or cushions stacked at knee height (Level 3), the first requirement is proper club selection.

For average-sized adults a club roughly 30 to 35 inches in length is recommended for a ball set at knee height. "Here I have chosen a U.S. Kids Golf blue 7-iron – about $20 to $25 at most golf discount stores, " says Don. "Junior clubs are very light, so if you prefer a heavier club you can cut down an old 6-iron and have a new grip installed for about $5 to $10 at most golf repair shops."

When doing this drill at home, instead of using real golf balls, you may want to use plastic or foam practice balls. Even wadded up pieces of paper will work. Initial muscle training begins with hitting into a practice net or even an old sheet hung from the ceiling to serve as a net.

A Place a practice ball on the rubber tee and begin by learning to let the ball "get in the way" of your new swing. Don't be too concerned with poor contact during your initial hitting sessions. In fact, you may have to practice quite diligently to make even moderate contact.

B Work slowly and meticulously relying on the broad array of drills from earlier chapters. (In the early stages of your elevated practice, don't try to hit the ball. Instead, just try to "tick" it, making it barely wiggle and fall off the tee. This is a test to see if you are able to make contact with your intended target at this elevated level.)

Chapter 11

Rounding 3rd and Heading for Home

TECHNIQUES TO KEEP YOUR SWING ON-PLANE AND INSIDE-OUT

Congratulations, you have completed all the drills necessary to begin ball striking and swing training routines designed to groove and completely program your body and mind with your new, powerful *Baseball Golf* swing! In baseball terms, you're rounding third base and heading for home. In both baseball and golf terms, you're about to score!

Before you head for the links, however, you need to continue to work from an elevated tee for a while to fully develop your new swing and to keep from reverting to your old one. You will work through a series of nine training routines. Treat each (A-I) as a pre-requisite for the next. Just as in school, you must graduate from each level by doing the assigned homework. Use a rubber tee for every ball you hit while working your way down to the ground. Along the way you will discard the shortened iron for one of regular length (C).

"When you set up, make your backswing and your follow-through, and hope the ball gets in the way of your swinging clubhead. Yes, I said hope," says Don. "Hope is the proper frame of mind to have. Hope implies the proper combination of trust and concentration. If you concentrate too hard, you may become too ball-oriented, causing you to lose connection with your newly programmed swing fundamentals.

Transitional Training Routines

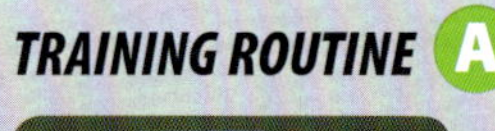

LEVEL 3

Practice three sets hitting 75 balls in each set.

Arrange the cushions at level 3, about knee high.
You can do the consecutive set in one day or on different days.

Before you head for the links, you need to continue to work from an elevated tee for a while to keep from reverting to your old swing.

"Many of my students become frustrated too soon in this stage of practicing. Some ask me to watch as they resort to using a shorter arm slap at the ball, which results in solid contact, but short flight. Then they say something like, 'Look, I can hit it solid like that. All I need to learn now is how to hit it farther.'"

"I've also had the opposite occur with students who have had success hitting the ball with distance using a very long and aggressive swing, which produces longer but very errant shots. These students, too impatient to work with their new swings, often revert to old techniques and rejoice at how much farther the ball is traveling. They tend to say something like, 'See, all I have to learn now is how to hit it straight!'

"In both instances, all I can say is: Don't ruin your new swing." emphasizes Don. "Stick to the program. Any attempt to hit the ball with a different swing slows your progress and throws you back into your old, inappropriate muscle firing patterns."

Follow the training routines, and you will be rewarded with a repeatable, athletic swing.

SWING **NOTE!** ***Levels change, but the feel doesn't.***

"Your arms, hands, and club swing the same at all levels in these routines. The only recognizable changes should be in the angle of your spine as you address the ball, and the plane of your arms as your spine tilts forward. At knee level, your arms will be thrown out more to meet the ball, while at ground level, your arms will be thrown down to meet the ball. Believe it or not, these swings should *feel* exactly the same because you should be using the same muscles in all cases.

TRAINING ROUTINE B

LEVEL 2

Practice three sets hitting 75 balls in each set.

Remove a box or cushion so your "hitting table" is now at level 2, about halfway between the knees and ankles.

TRAINING ROUTINE C

LEVEL 1

Practice three sets hitting 75 balls in each set.

Continue the same process at level 1, about ankle height. Use a normal length club. Choking down on a mid-range iron, such as a six or seven, is recommended.

TRAINING ROUTINE D

OFF A TEE

Practice three sets hitting 75 balls in each set.

Repeat the process at ground level off a tee (with no boxes or cushions).

TRAINING ROUTINE E

OFF THE GROUND

Practice three sets hitting 75 balls in each set.

Repeat the process at ground level (without a tee).

TRAINING ROUTINE 

ALTERNATE

Now that we've reached ground level, continue by alternating between the ground without a tee, the ground with a tee, and levels 1 and 2. Hit 20 balls at each of these four heights, beginning with the ground and working your way up for two successive sessions. Then work your way down to the ground in the third session.

PRACTICE, PRACTICE, PRACTICE

TRAINING ROUTINE G

Hit 25 balls at ankle height, 25 balls off a tee, and 25 balls off the ground – for one session only.

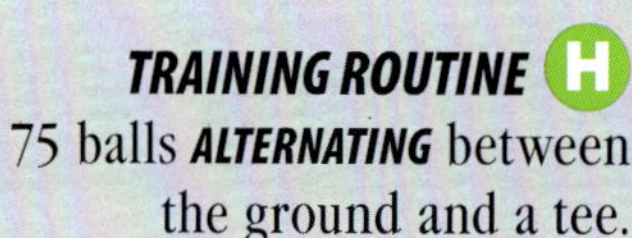

TRAINING ROUTINE H

Hit 75 balls ***ALTERNATING*** between the ground and a tee.

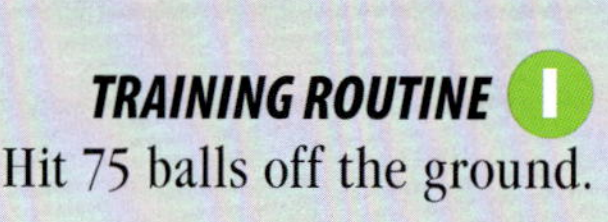

TRAINING ROUTINE I

Hit 75 balls off the ground.

After completing the training routines, spend some additional time on the driving range before scheduling a game on the course. Now that you have completed a series of drills and used verbal cues to acquire your new swing, you can't carry all of them with you onto the golf course. Your mind and body have been trained to think of only two things: "Stretch back" and "Spring through."

At the same time, the drills and cues remain valuable allies as you continue to practice on the range and refine your game. They can also serve as reminders when things go wrong. Hopefully, you will even develop your own ways to use what you've learned to positively influence your game.

For example, one of Don's students, an avid baseball fan, has had great success using the image from The Opposite Field Drill to help him hit more fairways and greens. He simply visualizes a baseball diamond while going through his pre-shot routine and swings fearlessly toward the opposite field gap.

When done properly, his muscles relax; He strikes the ball with authority down the fairway and onto the green in ways he never did before. This student has come to trust that when you're playing golf, the rough, the woods, and water that lurk beyond the fairways are nothing more than the opposite outfield gap. By relaxing his muscles and swinging inside-out in the direction of the gaping rough or

For the best results repeat routines G, H and I twice more before taking your new swing out to the practice range and, later, the golf course.

The drills and cues remain valuable allies as you continue to practice on the range and refine your game. They can also serve as reminders when things go wrong.

bottomless lake, he is confident that his new swing and golf club design will work together to centrifugally draw his ball naturally away from the hazards and into the fairway.

You should feel free to experiment and use your own imagination to come up with ways to continue to refine and groove your new swing.

Your new swing will produce a natural draw, a ball flight that curves right-to-left for right-handed golfers, and left-to-right for left-handed golfers. Depending on foot alignment and grip variables, you might produce a very slight, powerful fade. If you are slicing, turn directly to page 134 for more help.

In order to build confidence in your new swing, avoid playing directly for score or in a match. Instead, schedule at least three "practice play" rounds of golf where your purpose for playing is to practice on the golf course. Set aside any expectations. Head to the course with an open mind. If you have had success in your practice sessions, try to recall those positive swings on the course even if it means teeing balls in the middle of the fairway.

Wedges

Irons

Woods

You should now be able to stand with correct posture and balance, transfer your weight correctly, and have a centrifugal release. By following these procedures, the bottom of your swing will occur somewhere between the center of your stance and your lead heel or under your lead shoulder (lead arm point of hinge). Without getting too technical we know shorter irons with more loft are struck more solidly and with more control if we place the ball just before the bottom of the swing arc, contacting the ball as the club is still descending. Therefore, ball placement with short irons is normally in the center of your stance. Ball position with each iron varies slightly (as shown) by moving the ball a little more forward and a little farther away as each iron increases in length (1/2 inch) and decreases in loft.

A NOTE OF CAUTION

Pop Your Own Balloon

Once you begin to hit golf balls outside and on the course, tension might tend to creep back into your muscles. This will cause you to lose consistency and produce erratic results. It is sometimes very easy for Don to spot students whose muscles are tight. Sometimes, however, tension is not as visible. "I like to tell my students to picture their muscles as a balloon and "pop" the balloon," says Don. "When all the air goes out of the balloon, you will feel all the tension rush out of your muscles, especially those in your arms, hands, and shoulders!"

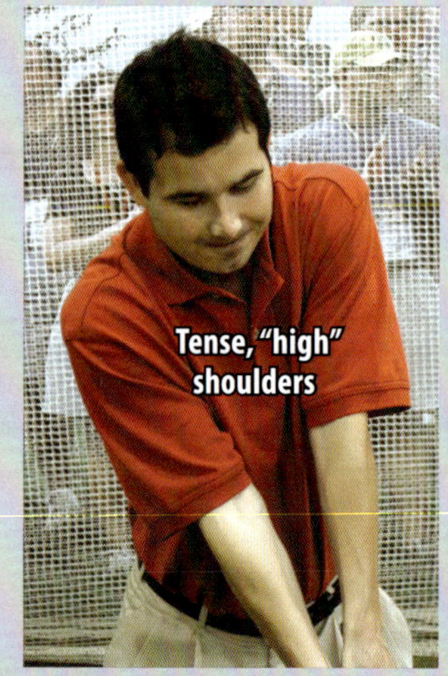

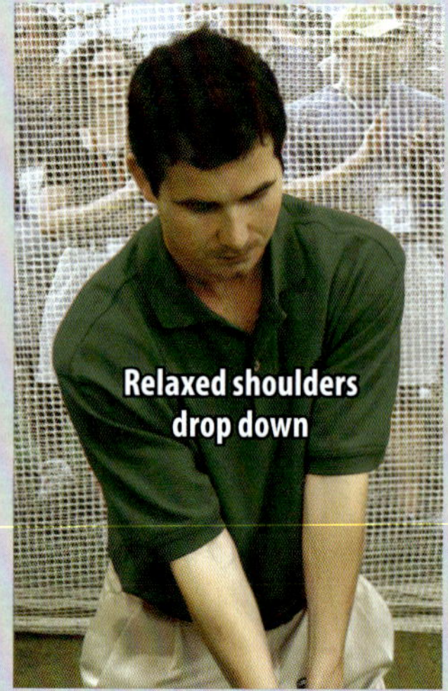

One school of thought suggests that it doesn't matter how you swing, as long as you arrive at impact in a good position as shown here. "While there's some merit to this belief, I would argue that how you swing *does* matter," says Don. "Sure, unorthodox, odd, or bad swings can produce good shots, and even good impact positions – especially if you're a pro who practices almost every day for hours at a time. But for the average golfer, how you swing is very important.

"Golf is ultimately a game of misses. The player with the 'best misses' will often find himself in position to win more often than most of his competitors. The Baseball Golf drills and training routines have expanded not only your golf-swing knowledge, but also your ability to more consistently arrive at impact in a good position to produce great shots and 'better misses.' Keep practicing this proven method, and you will become not just a better golfer, but the best golfer you can be.

Relax! Have fun. And, remember: Be the Pen and Rubber Band. Stretch back and Spring through.

Your new *Baseball Golf* model swing:

BACK VIEW – WOOD

BACK VIEW – IRON

FRONT VIEW – WOOD

This sequence of Don's long-time student and friend, Tom Haire, shows a perfect example of a baseball swing adapted for golf. "After several failed attempts with to make his swing more upright, Tom came to me," says Don. "Tom is without a doubt one of the straightest hitters I've ever played with or coached. Many times while playing a practice round on the course, Tom has hit three or four balls on a hole to work on his driving. Often when we arrived where the balls landed in the fairway, they were grouped so close together you could have thrown a blanket over them."

Although Mike Davie posed for most of the "incorrect" photos used in this book, in reality he is a top-notch teacher with an exceptional swing. As a result of his experience as a black belt in Karate, Mike realized *The Baseball Golf Swing Method* could supply him with the leverage he needed to increase his clubhead speed. It did. That increased speed was just what he needed to become a professional golfer.

Chapter 12

Extreme Concepts: **Unusual Tips for the Body and Mind**

THE BODY

When you finish working through this book and begin to play golf, you may unfortunately encounter recurring swing problems that impede improvement. Over the years I've developed a few extreme swing fixes for the body and mind that consistently help many of my students work through these roadblocks. I believe they will help you too.

The most common swing fault in golf occurs when pressure is applied from the trail arm and hand cupping the lead wrist and lead forearm. Photo ❶ demonstrates this weak and ineffective position, one that wreaks havoc in the world of golf. Photo ❷ demonstrates the correct position of my lead wrist in a muscle-balanced position. Cupping is such a huge problem that I've included three extreme fixes or remedies. Try each of these and maybe one will click for you as they have many times for my students.

HOODING THE CLUB AT THE TOP: Cupping is an improper manipulation in the hands resulting in a "bent" lead wrist and an open clubface at the top of your swing. Hooding is the opposite manipulation of the hands resulting in an "arched" lead wrist and a closed clubface at the top of your swing. To "unbend" your lead wrist, practice "hooding" the club as in ❸. From your address position, with the club behind the ball, start swinging the club back as you have learned. Focus on closing the clubface and arching your lead wrist as you near the top of your swing. Swing easily for the first few passes, because this type of take-away can cause strain. Keep in mind this is a temporary training technique used only to improve the position of your hands and wrists at the top of your swing. This top-of-the-swing position may remind you of the swings of Bruce Lietzke, Lee Trevino, or Jim Furyk.

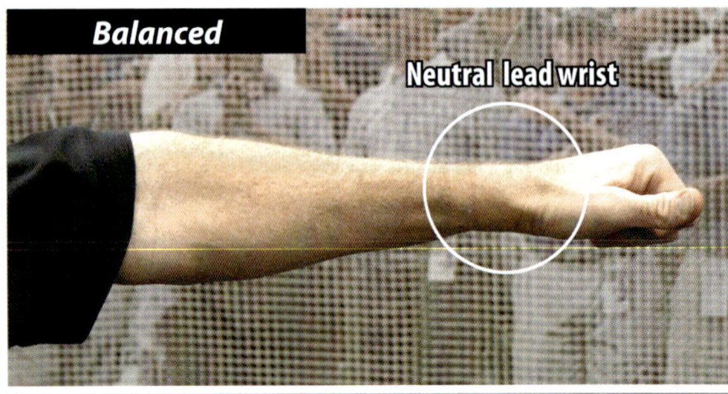

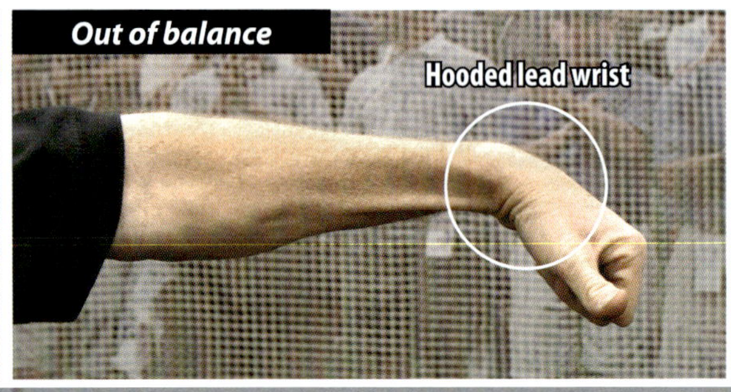

THE TRAY POSITION: Changes in the swing can be difficult because we have muscle groups on our lead side, and muscle groups on our trail side. Often, we must try one or the other to determine how best to make a positive change. "Hooding" the club as you have just read, is Dons way of overpowering the trail wrist by 'empowering' the lead wrist. The Tray Position, however, focuses directly on relaxing the trail wrist. Learn to bend the trail wrist back by imagining you are holding a tray at the top of your swing. Notice how your trail elbow points "in" toward your torso rather than out. Notice also how your trail palm feels "up" as if pointing toward the sky. By relaxing the trail wrist and learning to bend it back – your lead wrist automatically flattens and squares the clubface at the top of the swing.

Trail hand feels as if it is on top of lead hand

Lead hand reaches over trail hand...

... collapsing the trail wrist and elbow

EXTEND THE LEAD ARM OVER THE TRAIL ARM: This is an excellent exercise to place your arms and hands in the correct position at the top of your swing. In many students, the trail side dominates – getting on top of the lead arm to begin the downswing. To teach the trail side to be more passive, sometimes it is necessary to take control with your lead side. Try reaching on your backswing. Feel as if your lead arm and wrist are reaching over the top of your trail arm and wrist. You may combine this thought with the tray position. Avoid over-straining. I can't express how important I believe this drill is. When you practice extension, remember to reach out, never up!

CLOSE YOUR SHOULDERS DRASTICALLY: Okay, now that we've stopped the dreaded cupping of the lead wrist, let's attack the slice with another extreme tip designed to focus only on your swing path. If you are still slicing, chances are your path is still outside-in. (See pg. 70 & pg. 90.) Even after working through this book, you may be unable to produce the inside-out path you need to centrifugally close the clubface and stop the slice. When this happens the best thing to do is take correction to the extreme by drastically closing your shoulders as shown. Take your normal stance, then, without moving the position of your feet, adjust your shoulders so you feel as if they are pointing 20 yards to the right of your target (20 yards left for left-handed players). It is OKAY to feel as if your lead shoulder is very high and your trail shoulder is very low. When hitting, you may feel more comfortable playing the ball farther back in your stance, but try to avoid playing the ball too close to your trail foot. Keep the ball just in front of the center of your stance to provide the desired results.

SWING SMALL, GRIP LIGHT: Many times it seems as if I need to beg my students to relax their grip pressure. To my continued bewilderment, they continue to squeeze the grip during their swing. I believe this is due to the natural tendency to attempt to generate clubhead speed with muscles in the arms, hands, and shoulders. If you continually hit the ball to the far right or, if you slice terribly, try this. Hold the club as lightly as possible. Your fingers will be closed, but your wrists will feel "sloppy," hinging and unhinging more than normal. Begin slowly to keep from swinging too hard. Let short swings gradually increase until you reach waist high. Feel the clubhead open and close as you swing back and through. Your weight should transfer as if you were tossing a ball underhand. Practice hitting balls from a high tee; make sure you swing through only to waist high, hitting the ball very short distances. Keep in mind the benefits of this drill can only be realized if you practice the drill without trying to swing through to a full finish.

SHORTEN YOUR ARM SWING: One of the most frequent problems I see is over-swinging. Most golfers who over-swing are oblivious to the fact that they are doing it. When asked, most feel they are inflexible or too tight to make a full swing and reach parallel on their backswing. With the use of video, I can show them how their swings break down due to their attempts to get the club back as far as they can. What is the purpose of the backswing? We all pull the club back to torque our large muscles to create sufficient power to come forward. In my opinion, over-swingers coil poorly. Then, they have to pull back with their arms to try to find the power lost by not coiling properly.

Refer back to Chapter 5: The Windup and the Coil. In this chapter we told you that by making a tight body coil and turning your shoulders fully, you would reduce the need to incorrectly use your arms in an attempt to lengthen your back swing and create more power. You simply shorten your arm motion instead. The stretch you feel when coiling properly widens your swing and lengthens it even though you've shortened the swinging of your arms. Train this way for a few buckets, and you will go from feeling powerless to feeling as if you can now "crush" the ball with your hips.

KEEP YOUR ARMS DOWN: Picking the arms up too fast on the backswing is another very common problem that requires more than one possible cure. As you've read throughout the course of this book, lifting the arms can cause sway in the hips and tilt in the spine. Most often, golfers who lift the club abruptly during their backswing, cut across the ball on their downswing creating a slice. To break this "lifting" habit, try placing a small towel under your lead arm. Tuck it securely into your arm pit. Make a few practice swings without allowing the towel to fall. You will immediately notice the need to turn your shoulders in order to keep your lead arm in position to hold the towel. This connection helps eliminate the lift of the arms by training the larger shoulder and back muscles to move first. Your arms will feel as if they are down instead of up. Feel free to hit balls with the towel under your arm, you should be able to take a three quarter swing. You will feel quite powerful with a much shorter swing. If you don't have a small towel, a head cover or golf glove works just as well. Vijay Singh often spends hours hitting balls using this very concept.

To demonstrate an important concept that is sure to help you with your slice, position yourself on the side of a hill with the ball above your feet at least a foot. Picture a downswing motion that descends down the hill that is in front of you. Then, think exactly the opposite, and picture your club and swing path traveling up the hill as you swing through the ball. Your swing will immediately take on an inside-out path. With a little practice your release will occur on time and with less effort.

Begin swinging "up" the hill by taking very short backswings, about waist high. If you have ever played or watched tennis the swing would look and feel like a simple tennis forehand.

SWING NOTE! *Help for slicers.*

"Over the years I've accumulated rooms full of teaching equipment including high speed video, medicine balls, punch bowls, mirrors, tee-balls, broom handles – the list goes on and on," says Don. "Someone once asked me what I'd do if I couldn't use all my gadgets and equipment. While I know I can do a better job training people with the equipment, I could get by as long as I have my hill or my boxes."

GETTING BACK ON-PLANE: The more I teach and work on instruction concepts, the less I play! Unfortunately, I wasn't in practice when the first set of pictures for this book was taken. However, something good came out of something bad. This picture shows my swing just a little off-plane – a common fault that crept back into my swing. I returned to keeping my club on-plane, and you can too. To keep your club on-plane during this part of the backswing, try pushing down with your hands and/or lead shoulder to begin your swing away from the ball. By pushing down you can affect the clubhead and shaft just as a teeter-totter on a play ground works – when one side goes down, the other side must go up!

HIT THE OTHER BALL: While major breakthroughs in your golf game might occasionally come from experimenting with different feels or positions, most often they'll occur by altering/changing an old concept, image or perception. Here is a prime example of a personal breakthrough that helped my shoulder turn and coil when I created a mental picture of a second ball and alternative target. To visualize and experience it for yourself, lay tow clubs on the ground to simulate these actual and imagined target lines and ball positions. During your back swing from the actual ball (**A**) switch your focus to the imaginary ball (**B**) and pretend you want to hit it down the imagined target line, behind you and perpendicular to the actual target line. Then on the downswing, refocus on the actual ball (**A**) and hit it in the direction of the real target.

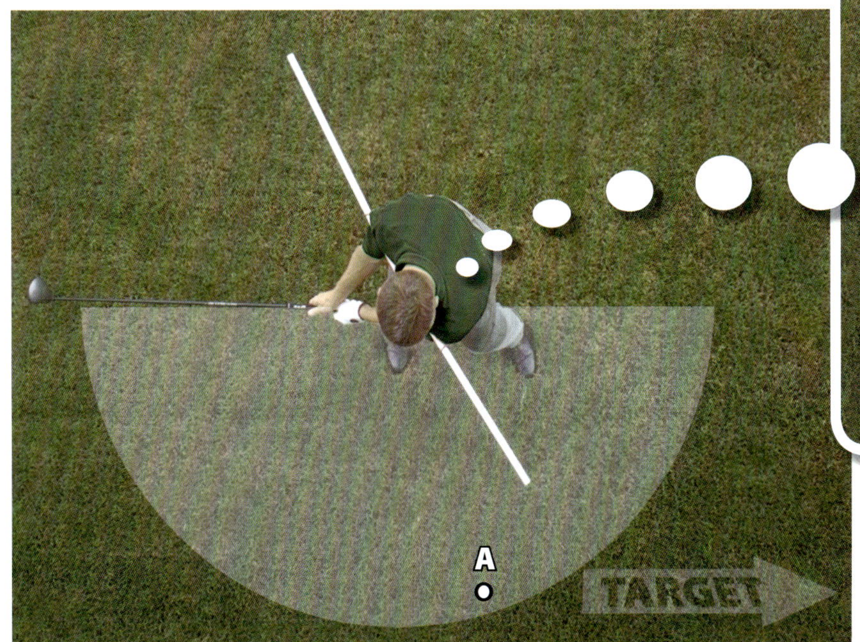

THE MIND

For years teachers and golfers have talked about how important the mind is in golf. Yet, for some reason they seem to think the muscles are better for doing what the mind is meant to do. Many teachers instruct students to groove their swing, so they will eventually develop a repeatable motion using muscle memory. But, this is not possible. First, you cannot "groove" your swing simply by repeating it over and over. If that were the key to success in golf, we would all be pros! Second, muscles don't remember. The mind remembers. Muscles do only what the mind tells them to do. It is the mind that can remember and transfer motion memory to the muscles. Motion memory, not muscle memory, is what gives us the ability to repeat our swings.

As a teenager, I remember feeling distracted by thoughts that interfered with my concentration while trying to hit important shots, particularly when someone was watching. I always blamed poor shot making on my inability to learn a consistent swing. I also learned that it does not matter how great your swing is if you can't recall it when you need it.

It does not matter how great your swing is if you do not understand how to recall it so you can depend upon it in casual play and competition.

Realizing that muscles don't remember helped me to understand why some players, many of whom do not possess scientifically sound and consistent swings, still manage to hit perfect shots under pressure. All these players possess a strong degree of concentration. This intensity helps them lock into memory the swing that needs to be made at that particular moment.

This concept helps to explain the differences among talented players in the pro ranks. Many of golf's elite are known to possess superior mental capabilities, often surpassing their physical capabilities. Ben Hogan reportedly had a genius-level IQ. Bobby Jones was a noted scholar who attended Harvard. Tom Watson is a psychology graduate from Stanford. These men have succeeded in the academic and business world as well as on the fairways, largely because they can control their thoughts and focus on the task at hand.

I am not a golf psychologist, but what I've experienced over time will show you how to control the mental side of golf. I believe that three things are required: relaxation, imagery, and recall.

I remember my first experience with a sports psychologist. It was a beautiful Florida day – perfect for golf, and there I was stuck inside all day. Not only was I trapped inside all day, but I also had to endure mental exercises instead of having fun on the course. My feeling could be summed up by one phrase: "This is a bunch of bull!" The outcome, however, sent me away with a whole new way of looking at my game.

Now, this may sound a bit too "New Age" for some of you, but bear with me. To begin, the instructor had our class sit in comfortable positions on couches and told us to breathe in slowly through our noses and out through our mouths. We concentrated on relaxing individual muscle groups to release tension from our bodies. Then, we listened through earphones to several relaxation tapes. I found myself relaxing, but not falling asleep. Still awake, I began daydreaming that I was someplace else. The imagery was vivid. I actually felt I was in that other place. My imagination had taken control of my thoughts. The power of my mind was both relaxing me and transporting me to another place entirely. Hey, I thought this could really help my golf game! If I can learn to mentally transport myself somewhere relaxing when I am on the golf course under pressure, it may help me relax enough to hit the shot well.

At first, I tried to relax and imagine what the shot I was facing felt like when I previously and successfully executed it. This approach seemed to work best for me while putting, chipping, or pitching. Since these are shorter shots with a much simpler technique, they are easier to recall. It took me a little longer to be able to imagine the feel of my full swing technique.

It is a well known fact that negative thoughts diminish athletic performance, no matter what the sport. I had often heard and read about replacing negative thoughts with positive ones to improve performance. After attending the sports psychologist's seminar, I knew exactly how to do that – by relaxing and imagining I was somewhere else whenever I felt pressure on the golf course. I soon had a chance to put my newfound knowledge to the test for something besides putts, chips, and pitches.

While working as a pro at Pelican's Nest in Naples, Florida, I was often in match play with other pros at the club. During my matches, the sixth hole always seemed to give me trouble. It was a relatively short hole, about 330 yards with water on both sides of a narrow fairway. The shot required an accurate iron off the tee. I had hit about 9 of the previous 10 tee shots straight into the water, trying everything from a 1-iron to a 4-iron to no avail.

One evening while playing alone, I decided to practice my "mental imagery" as I was preparing to hit that shot. I was trying to picture a place where I wouldn't feel the anxiety I always felt on this hole. I imagined that I was back home on the farm in Illinois where I grew up hitting balls from my backyard into cornfields. I looked down at the ball and back up again to my target. Instead of seeing two intimidating bodies of water, I envisioned the cornfield and corner fencepost I had always aimed for in Illinois. As I prepared to make the shot, I could almost hear my mother yelling from the front porch, "Donny, don't you take any more divots out of my yard!"

I think you get the picture. By occupying my mind with familiar, comforting thoughts of home, I completely forgot about the pressure and my ingrained fear of the water hazards on this hole. I tricked my mind. The result was a solid shot right down the middle, along with a new perspective on dealing with pressure. If you don't like the shot you are faced with, or do not feel comfortable on a particular hole, then take yourself out of that uncomfortable situation by "tricking" your mind.

Whether you're choking on the first tee in the Club Championship or playing for $10 with a pal, negative thinking can hurt your performance. More often than not, the pressure causes you to freeze and ultimately swing at the ball while your mind is panicking. Next time, try to trick your mind by visualizing yourself in a place where you always hit your best shots.

For me, that's back on a farm in Illinois. For you, it could be your backyard, a hole you always play well, or a driving range you like. It doesn't matter where you go, as long as you daydream yourself out of an uncomfortable situation into a comfortable, positive one. Try it; it works.

Don Peterson

A long time member of the Professional Golfers Association of America, Don has been playing and teaching golf for more than 35 years. His vast experience and love for the game of golf have helped him develop a unique style of teaching which has proven to be effective for golfers of all skill levels. The drills compiled and presented in this book reflect not only a deep understanding of the golf swing but also the knowledge and insight of a great teacher.

Don's students range from "first time" beginners to PGA touring pros. Through the years Don has worked with British Open Champion Todd Hamilton, comedian Jeff Foxworthy, NFL legend Brett Farve, and many of the Atlanta Braves. When not teaching, Don travels the country providing swing analysis and corporate golf entertainment for Fortune 500 companies including Anheuser-Busch and R.J. Reynolds.

Phil Nero

A talented journalist and author, Phil Nero is as passionate about golf as he is about words and storytelling. While he developed a smooth and precise writing style over the years, his golf game was anything but. Several years ago he began researching the similarities between the baseball and golf swings in what he describes as "a somewhat successful attempt to improve my game." During that time he met Don Peterson, whose book he helped refine and develop. Phil's new novel, *Twice Upon a Time*, has a fall 2007 publication date.